The
Warwickshire
Village Book

THE VILLAGES OF BRITAIN SERIES

Other counties in this series include

The Warwickshire Village Book

Compiled from the Warwickshire
Federation of Women's Institutes from notes
and illustrations sent by Institutes in the County

Published jointly by
Countryside Books, Newbury
and the WFWI, Leamington Spa

Countryside Books
3 Catherine Road
Newbury, Berkshire

ISBN 1 85306 032 1

Cover photograph of Ladbroke
taken by Mrs K. Telford

Produced through MRM Associates, Reading
Typeset by Acorn Bookwork, Salisbury, Wiltshire
Printed in England by J. W. Arrowsmith Ltd, Bristol

Foreword

Welcome to 'leafy' Warwickshire in the heart of England, through which the river Avon runs.

The county stretches from the Cotswolds in the south to Staffordshire in the north, and is bounded also by Oxfordshire, Northamptonshire, Leicestershire, the West Midlands and Worcestershire.

Warwickshire is rich in history with its Roman road, its own great battle at Edgehill in 1642, and the shades of the armies that marched across it to fight at Evesham in 1265 and Bosworth in 1485.

The County has three castles, at Maxstoke, Kenilworth and, of course, Warwick, this last being the finest medieval castle in the British Isles. There are also many fine houses from Compton Wynyates and Ragley Hall to the smaller Packwood House, Baddesley Clinton and the cottage near Stratford-upon-Avon where Anne Hathaway lived.

William Shakespeare must be Warwickshire's most famous son, but we also take pride in the novelist George Eliot, and Joseph Arch who founded the first trade union of farm workers.

Within this book you will read of the richly diverse villages which make up the beautiful County of Warwickshire. Members of the Federation have undertaken many hours of patient and willing research to produce this indispensable guide to our county. We know that all the contributors have derived a sense of achievement and enjoyment from their task, and we hope all who read the result will share our pleasure in this book.

Wendy Dillon
County Chairman

Acknowledgements

The Warwickshire Federation of Women's Institutes would like to thank all those members and their Institutes who have worked so hard to research and provide information and drawings for their villages. Also a special thank you to Joan Ellis, co-ordinator for the project.

County of WARWICKSHIRE

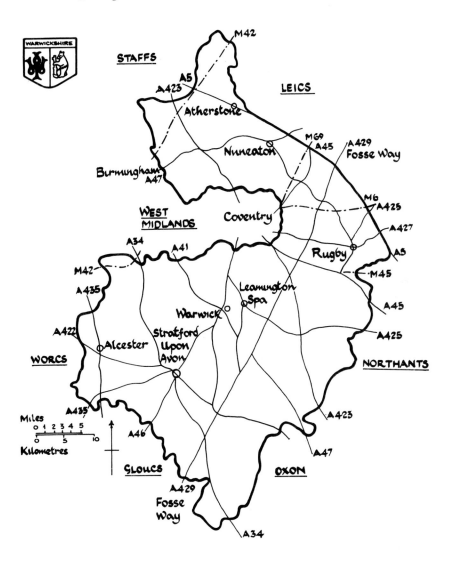

STAFFS

LEICS

A5
A423

M42

Atherstone

Nuneaton

M69
A45

A429
Fosse Way

Birmingham
A47

M6
A425

Coventry

A427

WEST
MIDLANDS

A34

A41

Rugby

A5

M42

M45

A435

Leamington
Spa

A422

Warwick

Stratford
Upon
Avon

A45

Alcester

A425

WORCS

NORTHANTS

A423

A435

A47

Miles
0 1 2 3 4 5

0   5   10
Kilometres

A46

GLOUCS

OXON

A429
Fosse
Way

A34

Alderminster Church

Alderminster ✑

Standing astride the busy A34 Stratford–Oxford road, Alderminster must be a familiar sight to the many travellers who pass through at speed.

The church was founded by a community of monks led by St Aegis and sent from Glastonbury in AD 530. After his death in 582 his shrine was a place of pilgrimage until suppressed by the Archbishop of Canterbury in 673. The community was taken over by Malmesbury Abbey, then Pershore Abbey who made it a house 'for maintenance of hospitality and for infirm monks'. At the same time an extension was made for a parish church of the Holy Cross and High Altar of St Mary Minster-Chancel, dedicated on 14th July 1286 by the Lord Bishop of Worcester.

The main part of the village was then at the top of the hill to the north-east, but in 1348 the Black Death wiped out most of the inhabitants, and those remaining grouped their homes near the church.

During the Civil War in 1642 Cromwellian troops were stationed in the village before the Battle of Edgehill. While renovation was going on in one of the older houses a walled-up body was found wearing a Roundhead breastplate.

In 1823 it was decided to build a tramway between Stratford-upon-Avon and Moreton-in-the-Marsh following the main road through Alderminster. A bridge was built over the Avon and the road at Alderminster was straightened so that it only had one track to cross. The day of opening, 5th September 1826, saw a crowd of thousands and celebrations at Moreton.

As there were several hills on the way, and horses were used to pull the tram, a halt was called at the top while the horse was unhitched and placed on the tram. The brake was released and then the whole load careered downhill to the bottom, where normal transport was resumed. The tramway was closed by the GWR in 1869.

During the 1870s a local landowner built 24 houses, the school and schoolhouse in the village. The school, which opened in 1872, was in use until 1971 when due to the retirement of the two teachers it was closed.

In 1960 about 100 houses were spread along the main road with a garage, post office/store, bakery and The Bell Inn. An ex-army hut was used as a village hall but a new Hall was built in 1963.

Since then many new houses have been built and the number of residents has almost doubled. At the same time the post office/stores and bakery have both closed, so villagers must visit Newbold or Stratford for pensions, stamps and food of all kinds. The old school sells architectural antiques (old baths, bricks and fireplaces) while The Bell Inn has become a bistro and restaurant.

Alvecote 🌿

Alvecote is a mining village. The mining of coal here in the 19th and 20th centuries has left a legacy of terraced houses, a spoil tip and, when it became flooded due to mining subsidence, the 'Alvecote Pools'. These are now a nature reserve and a Site of Special Scientific Interest, a haven for many uncommon insects, some rare plants and a great many birds.

Alvecote Priory, of which the ruins remain beside the Coventry canal, was a Benedictine priory founded in 1159. Its 14th century remains include a fine moulded doorway and a dovecote. It is now a picnic area.

The priory has an interesting legend attached to it. It was founded by a William Burdett and the legend says that he returned from a pilgrimage to the Holy Land to be told of his wife's infidelity. He killed her in anger, and later, having discovered the tale to be untrue, he founded the priory as a penance.

Arrow 🌿

Nowadays the traffic thunders out of the old Roman town of Alcester on the A422 and rushes off to Evesham and the world beyond and thus you miss Arrow, for the little village straddles this busy highway.

It is an old village, and until recent years was owned by the Marquis of Hertford who still lives in the village at Ragley Hall. Its main inhabitants in those early days were the employees and retired workers from the estate, but the social climate has changed now, and the great estates do not employ a large staff as of old. These days new houses are being built and old ones converted for the folks who commute into nearby towns.

The beautiful fertile land is farmed by the Marquis, and sheep and cattle graze beside woodland alive with deer and pheasant. All around neat hedgerows and well tilled fields give notice of the richness of the land and the careful attention it receives.

On the banks of the river Arrow is an old water mill which, until 25 years ago, was still grinding corn. The original mill was mentioned in the Domesday Book and dates back to 766. The setting is still beautiful and the millwheel still turns, although now it is part of an hotel restaurant.

Upriver from the Mill is Arrow church, a 12th century Norman church which is still lovingly cared for, although the adjacent rectory and coach-house are now private dwellings.

The boundary between Alcester and Arrow is Spittle Brook, and here there is a waterman's cottage and, still in the garden, below the old reservoir, a waterwheel, one of the oldest metal wheels in England, which operated to supply Alcester, 1½ miles away.

Beloved of many generations of children is the 'Elephant' tree! Set in the bank, just beyond the waterman's cottage, is the great trunk of an ancient oak tree which has grown to have all the texture and shape of an elephant. How many childhood fantasies must have been woven to explain his presence there! Sadly, the tree and the waterwheel are both threatened by future development plans.

At the junction between the Worcester and Evesham roads there is a toll house built in the 1850s, which could control both roads and collect tolls for the Marquis from the travellers with their livestock.

On the Worcester Road at this junction lived the wheelwright, and opposite was the forge and the blacksmith's cottage. As the motor car became king the enterprising wheelwright opened a garage, but even this has gone now, and a new house has taken its place. The schoolhouse, which was built in the mid 19th century, and the village shop have both closed, the former being offices.

Ragley Hall, set in rolling parkland, has a commanding position and comes unexpectedly into view in all its grandeur when travelling from Stratford or Worcester. The Hall and park are open to the public, with nature walks and an adventure playground for the children. There is a heronry in Ragley Park, and early mornings will catch a group of herons on the river bank, like old men chatting about the weather.

The Marquis tells this story of the Arrow Ghost. 'There is a spring on the main road betwen Arrow and Dunnington at the foot of Ragley Park. Towards the end of the 19th century travellers in coaches often saw a little old lady beside the spring begging a lift towards the village of Dunnington. Those who gave her a lift invariably found that she had disappeared when they stopped at Dunnington Crossroad to let her out of the carriage. Eventually someone had the idea of digging around the spring, and they found the bones of an old lady. The bones were reburied in Arrow churchyard in about 1900 and the ghostly old lady was never seen again.'

Aston Cantlow

Aston Cantlow is a village situated 7 miles north of Stratford-upon-Avon. The name is derived from the Norman, Cantelupe, which was the name of the baron who built a castle on the outskirts of the village in 1205. Now, sadly, only a few ridges in a field remain near the river Alne. The baron's son, Thomas, born in 1218, became famous as Chancellor of England during the reign of Henry III and following his death in 1282 was canonised by the Pope. Apart from St Augustine, Aston Cantlow is the only parish in England to claim a former vicar as a saint.

The church of St John the Baptist in Aston Cantlow is quite beautiful and the most important event here was in 1557 when William Shakespeare's parents were married. Their first child was baptised here in 1558. Shakespeare's mother, Mary Arden, lived in Wilmcote and his father, John Shakespeare, lived in nearby Snitterfield.

Aston Cantlow today has about 500 inhabitants, earning their living mainly in the neighbouring towns and cities as opposed to earning a living from the land as would have been the case 100 years ago.

Within the parish are the hamlets of Newnham, Shelfield, Little Alne, Billesley and Pathlow which lies on the A34.

Billesley was once owned by the Trussells, a family who lived for centuries in Billesley Manor which is now an hotel. The last Trussell was hanged in the time of Queen Elizabeth I as a highwayman. The village itself no longer exists as such, having been destroyed by the ravages of the Black Death in the Middle Ages, the only remains being a few humps in a field near the church of All Saints which is now redundant and closed, opening for only one or two services a year.

Aston Cantlow has a very fine medieval Guild Room opposite The Kings Head Inn. The Guild Hall is believed to have been the home of the Guild of St Mary, first mentioned in 1442, a religious guild which provided priests for the church services. This is now the Village Hall. Part of the Guild Hall used to be the village gaol. There was a chapel until the 1960s in Chapel Lane with visiting preachers, one of whom was nicknamed 'I be Charlie'. He used to say, 'I be Charlie and I comes from Binton'. Another fascinating character in the history of Aston Cantlow was George Lewing who was the first headmaster of the village school from 1847 until 1873. The school in Aston Cantlow was closed down in the 1960s.

In Mill Lane there was a mill, water powered, where they produced paper in 1748, needles in the 1800s, and then ball bearings for bicycles. This existed until the early 1960s. There was a brush factory in 1915.

The railway no longer exists in Aston Cantlow but signs of the old track can still be seen from the Halt.

Austrey 🐾

Austrey is a small village in the very north of the county, near junction 11 of the M42, 7 miles from Tamworth and 8 miles from Ashby-de-la-Zouch. Close by is Twycross Zoo and Market Bosworth, famous for the Battle of Bosworth Field in 1485 when Richard III was killed. Originally known as Alcestre, Austrey had a population of 335 in 1911. The census of 1981 showed the population had increased to 962.

New housing developments are much a part of the village today. Many farms have been sold, land has been absorbed by larger arable farmers and much of what for years had been rich pasture-land has now been turned to the plough. Several farmhouses have been sold off with just a few acres of land.

Throughout the village are many delightful old properties, one being the black and white Bishops Farm House, bearing the date 1521. Over the road stands a fine three storey Manor House. The intriguing Saddler's Cottage stands broadside to Warton Lane, and Farthings is a fine timbered property, part of which was once the village shop. Now standing across the road is a modern purpose-built general store and post office.

Built in 1808, the Baptist church stands just off the main road. Many slate headstones are still to be found around the car park. St Nicholas church looks down over the village, as it has done since the 13th century. The Old Vicarage is no longer occupied by the vicar of Austrey and Warton, who now lives in a modern house next door.

Close by is The Bird in Hand pub with its thatched roof and outside stands a medieval plinth, said to be the meeting place for those who sought work in years gone by. In 1897 a cross was erected on the top of the four octagonal stone steps, to commemorate the Diamond Jubilee of Queen Victoria.

Austrey Parochial School, erected in 1850 is now used as a village hall, since the opening of Austrey C of E first school in 1969.

As Austrey looks to the future, there are many reminders of the past, one of those being Windmill Lane at the top of which, naturally, there once stood a windmill. From here there is an almost panoramic view over parts of Leicestershire, Derbyshire, Staffordshire and Warwickshire.

The village now has a Ride and Drive School and it is not unusual to see a horse-drawn carriage passing by, drawn by four in hand. Many bridle paths encourage horse riding. For those who enjoy walking there are many routes to choose from, one popular walk being Cinder Lane, which encircles the village.

Barford

The river Avon meanders through Barford on its way to Wasperton, Charlecote and Stratford-upon-Avon. It is a lively village of undulating fields, cut in half by the noisy A429 with numerous little lanes where new houses stand beside old cottages.

Barford fathered Joseph Arch, who started the National Union of Agricultural Workers in 1872, went to Parliament as a Liberal MP, and who was born and died in the little cottage opposite the church. Every year agricultural workers make a pilgrimage to his grave in the churchyard, and one of the public houses bears his name.

Many inhabitants enjoy a stroll down Church Street, or along the Wellesbourne Road, to do their shopping at the thriving stores-cum-post office, where they can meet acquaintances and have a gossip. The old bakery is now a hairdresser's, and the blacksmith now, alas, practises his art from one of the nearby industrial estates and his forge has been converted into a house. But he and his forebears have left their mark on St Peter's church in the form of the weathervane and wrought iron gates.

The Mill, manufacturing animal feed, goes back many years and the huge lorries turn into and out of Mill Lane several times each day.

St Peter's church has a rector who is responsible also for the parishes of Wasperton, a little hamlet a mile along the Wellesbourne Road, and for Sherbourne, across the river. Sherbourne is more than a hamlet, with a magnificent church, built in the 1860s by a member of the Ryland family. The full peal of bells can be heard joyfully echoing across the water meadows on Friday evenings when bell practice is taking place, and again before service on Sunday mornings.

St Peter's Barford is proud of the fact that it has several times been awarded the coveted prize for Best Kept Churchyard in the diocese, and bears witness to many hours of hard work. The village in a similar competition has won the Best Kept Village award twice.

On the outskirts of the village lies Westham House, an elegant

15

building used during the last war as a girls school, and now as an adult education college. The mellow red brick reflects the sun, and the well-kept gardens are an ideal working place for the many aspiring artists who assemble for painting courses during the summer months.

This is very much tourist country, with Shakespeare and his links a mere 7 miles away. Although not a beautiful village in one sense of the word, all the gardens are bright with flowers and well-tended lawns and the village green, recreation ground and village hall are all neat and tidy. The hall is the memorial to the Lord Lieutenant's father who was killed during the war.

Barton-on-the-Heath

The village lies on the crest of a hill just inside the border of south Warwickshire, the name being derived from the word 'barton' meaning homestead. Over the centuries the heathland has been converted to agricultural use and today, of the 33 houses here, three are working farms. It was first recorded as far back as 1086, when Robert de Stafford was overlord of Barton Manors.

The main part of the village consists of a small triangular green, with a Memorial Well-house in its centre, encircled by several well kept Cotswold stone houses, a schoolhouse, a forge (the latter two now unfortunately unused) and the 17th century Barton Manor House. The Manor is a lovely stone built house and parts of it are thought to have been designed by the famous Inigo Jones, for some of the rooms bear the mark of his work.

The old school has closed, mostly because of the diminishing size of families, and is now used for an occasional meeting place for discussing matters of concern to the people of the village.

In the reign of James 1 there lived, in the house next to the old school-house, the famous lawyer Thomas Dover, the creator of the famous Dover Games which were held annually on Dover's Hill near Chipping Campden. These games, for many years extinct, are now held once more on the same spot as they were centuries ago.

To the west of Barton House stands the church of St Lawrence, a lovely part-Norman building with an unusual saddleback roof.

Today the faithful tread the path to worship, as did those in the days of the Tudors who, on passing the rectory, would place food in the wall of the house, for the sustenance of the two preists who lived there, caretakers of the church.

The Old Rectory is a part-Tudor, part-William and Mary building. Part of it was constructed from bricks, kilned only a few hundred yards from the site. Here there lived a lady by the name of Olivia Wilmot, who was married in the church by her uncle, the then rector of St Lawrence, to J. T. Serres, from whom she later parted. A great mystery surrounds this lady, for she claimed to have been the niece of George IV and the daughter of the Duke of Cumberland. These facts have never been authenticated, but she was a very talented water colour artist, becoming a landscape painter to the then Prince of Wales, and to the Court. Early this century The Old Rectory was a private preparatory school but in early 1940s it became once more a family home.

Barton cannot boast of having a village shop, but is fortunate in having several vans calling with a variety of foods, plus a regular delivery of milk, a good daily paper delivery, a library van which calls periodically and a good local post office.

Bearley 🌿

Bearley lies just off the A34, between Henley-in-Arden and Stratford-upon-Avon. It is spread over a wooded hillside, with several attractive farmhouses and cottages.

The church of St Mary is on the hill. It has been extensively rebuilt but some Norman work is still visible and it has a 15th century font.

The story of the Miller of Bearley is a local tale associated with Windmill Woods. The miller is said to guard his sacks of gold hidden under a millstone, which is all that remains of the old mill. The legend is that at midnight, when the moon is full, the miller takes his six horses to water, so leaving his hoard unattended. This is the only time when the daring youth of the village can attempt to raise the stone, but to date this has not been successful!

Bidford-on-Avon

Bidford-on-Avon, originally named Byda's Ford, dates back to Saxon times. The Roman legions tramped the Ryknild Street, part of which still bears the name. A large Anglo-Saxon burial ground was discovered in 1922 with a wonderful collection of jewels, shields, and other artifacts, dating back to AD 500.

The population has almost quadrupled during the last 50 years. Houses are going up at a very great rate and Bidford is in danger of becoming a small town. Consequently, gone are the kingfishers, jays, woodpeckers, herons and swans which used to be so much in evidence. Extensive work on the opening of the river for pleasure craft has much to answer for.

Before the Second World War practically all the men and women worked on the land, apart from a small handful of men who worked at a small brickyard (now defunct). Present day workers commute to nearby towns like Birmingham, Stratford and Coventry, although an expanding industrial estate is now well established and is employing a considerable work force.

There is only one historic building, the old Falcon Inn, dating from the 13th century. This has had a very chequered career over the years and was rescued from being a very run-down tenement a few years ago. It is now divided into flats, while still preserving its original form. Shakespeare was reputed to have got very drunk at the inn and slept off the effects beneath a crab-apple tree on the way home to Stratford. There was a tree on the spot until 1824, when it was removed in a 'decayed condition'. A replacement of the tree was planted in 1976, but unfortunately it was vandalised within a few weeks. Shakespeare's rhyme (see Temple Grafton), in which he refers to 'Drunken Bidford' is believed to list the various villages where he sampled the ales.

Bidford men were well known in the area for cockfighting, wrestling and backsword play. Bidford's Morris Men were exceptionally well known and performed at many local celebrations, even performing at the Royal Agricultural Hall in 1866. There was still a team in Bidford until a few years ago.

One of the highlights in Bidford's past was Trinity Monday,

when the High Street was filled with stalls following services at the parish church on Trinity Sunday. No one seems to be sure when this custom died out, but it was still going on in 1871.

The parish church of St Laurence is of great interest, the first incumbent being Rogenus Capellanno in 1260. There is some wonderful church plate, presented by the Duchess of Dudley in 1660.

Alas, there are no local 'characters' left. But this is a sign of the times, not peculiar to Bidford. The last blacksmith died recently and has not been replaced. No longer can the old women be seen on the river bank, stripping the withies for basket making – the withy beds have vanished!

Bilton ✥

Bilton is a village within the Borough of Rugby. The parish was mentioned in Domesday Book and the name is thought to be derived from Bell, being a stream on which the village stood, and Ton the old English meaning for village.

During the 19th century the village consisted of the church, village green, stocks and ancient cross. There were large estates and some farming land in the vicinity which provided employment for the village people. Now in the late 20th century the village is surrounded by built up areas, apart from the south which is still free from development.

As one approaches the village from Rugby, St Mark's church spire stands out. The church was rebuilt about 1350 and is an example of pure Gothic architecture. The late M. H. Bloxham, the celebrated antiquarian, said of St Marks – 'I have visited upwards of a thousand churches in this country and on the continent but have never been so much impressed as with the grand but quiet beauty of this small village church.'

Closely associated with St Marks and Bilton village are the Assheton family. They are the patrons of the living and three of the family have served as rectors. As a memorial to his wife Mr Orme Assheton built a Chapel of Ease where services could be held for those unable to walk as far as the church. Nearby, Mr Assheton erected 'The Magnet', a building to be used for social and recreational purposes to attract people away from the public houses. This building has now been converted into cottages, and the road parallel to Main Street is called Magnet Lane. The garden and playground at the corner of Church Walk were given by the Assheton family to the village for all time.

Joseph Addison (1672–1719), a distinguished poet and classical scholar, purchased Bilton Hall close by the church for £8,000 along with the Manor of Bilton. He married the Dowager Countess of Warwick and they had a daughter, Charlotte. Addison was buried in Westminster Abbey and Charlotte asked to be buried there as well, but as this was not possible she asked to be buried at midnight in St Mark's churchyard. This was carried out but her grave has never been found. Her ghost is said to haunt Bilton Hall.

The Church House is situated near the main road and the village. It serves as a village hall and behind it is the Warwickshire County Council Clinic serving many villages nearby.

Bilton Park was one of the very fine houses near the village and the Prince of Wales, later Edward VIII, played polo here.

Bilton Hall

Dominating the village green is The George Inn, an old coaching house and a distinctive three storey building. Behind was the village smithy, in use until after the First World War. The village stocks, last used in 1866 stand on the green, as well as a stone cross which may have been a preacher's open air pulpit or more probably a market cross.

Granny's Pie Shop, perhaps the oldest building in the street, has been restored. Its thatched roof has been replaced by tiles from the now demolished Holy Trinity Church in Rugby but the old timbered front has been retained. The main street is lined with a great variety of well stocked shops and there is an air of lively friendliness among the shoppers.

Two Wakes were held in Bilton: Crow Pie and Pindle Wake, the latter taking place in Pindle Field where all the fun of the fair took place including 'catching the greasy pig'. Older residents remember the village as a rural community with cows being driven down the main street to market.

Binley Woods

The village, unlike most, cannot lay claim to antiquity, for until 1961 the village of Binley Woods did not exist. However, the area has many historical associations, dating back to the Norman Conquest when the woods were 'half a mile long and a furlong broad'. The Cistercian monks of Coombe Abbey held here a Court Leet with gallows, and an Assize of Bread and Ale.

Situated on the south-east boundary of Coventry and the outskirts of the Borough of Rugby, the community that was to become Binley Woods began its modern development in the 1920s following the sale of the Coombe Abbey estates by the Earl of Craven. During the 1920s and 30s, people settled in the area, bought land and built homes. In the 1940s they were joined by homeless people from bombed Coventry, who fled to the comparative safety of Binley and lived in shacks, caravans and anything that could be called home.

Some of the original 'pioneering' families still live in the area, and it is they who can recall the days before tarmacadam, when visitors were advised to bring their wellies when they came to call. One elderly resident can remember the days when, if she wanted to go to town, she wore her wellies to the bus stop, left them behind a convenient hedge, and donned her shoes. On her return, the wellies were always waiting for her! Eventually the mud receded and the roads emerged, and the wellies could be consigned to the gardens. Gradually, over the years, residents came to enjoy the 'luxuries' of mains drainage, piped water, and when the old gas lights were considered to be too expensive (at £1.12s.6d per quarter!) they were replaced by electricity.

By the late 1950s the residents were anxious that the area should establish an identity of its own and no longer be confused with the neighbouring suburb of Coventry, known as Binley. Villagers were asked to vote, and the name of Binley Woods was adopted. Since then, the local people have worked hard to create a sense of community.

In 1987, Binley Woods made history when, through a Local Ecumenical Project – the first in Warwickshire – the church in Binley Woods was inaugurated.

It is a long time since the woods were 'half a mile long and a furlong broad' but at least the woods are still there. Saved from development through the efforts of a local group, the Friends of Brandon Wood, the village can now boast one of the first Community Woods in Europe, jointly managed by the Forestry Commission and the 'Friends'.

Bishops Itchington

Bishops Itchington lies on the B4551 between Kineton and Southam. The river Itchen meanders to the south and the village is overlooked by Burton Hills to the west.

The church of St Michael stands on high ground in the village and was built in the year 1872, on the site of the original church of All Saints. Already 36 years old at the time was the Congregational chapel, which was built in 1836. Today this is no longer a place of worship, but converted into a dwelling house. In 1856 a Primitive Methodist chapel was built and today, this building houses the village post office and general stores.

Houses in the village numbered 130 at the turn of the century. The population increased with the opening of the Greaves, Bull and Lakin Cement Works, who built homes for their employees and were responsible for the building of the Greaves Club and the Memorial Hall, both of which are still very much in use today.

Whilst quarrying for stone, dinosaur fossils were discovered, which are now housed in the Natural History Museum at South Kensington.

Years ago all water was obtained from the various village pumps, or wells. Wash days were very hard work, and bath night meant a zinc bath on the kitchen floor. Fresh bread was delivered to the door, as was milk, which came by pony and trap, and was measured out of a churn, straight into jugs.

The village did have a manor house, but unfortunately it is no longer in its original state having been rebuilt after being destroyed by fire. The wonderful buildings of the mansion sadly have gone, with all the history they held, which included visits from Queen Elizabeth I and Cromwell.

Many years ago the village had its own bus service to Leamington Spa, which was owned by Mr J. Edwards, affectionately known to everyone as 'Jimmy'. If Jimmy took 30 passengers to Leamington, he waited for 30 passengers to return to the village. The service is quite different today!

In 1949 the village was unable to form a parish council due to lack of interest from the men. Mrs Chapel Hyam, President of the WI at the time, and six of her members stood for election, together with one solitary man and they were all duly elected. This was a unique occasion, and received media attention under the title of 'The Petticoat Government' of Bishops Itchington.

Bishops Tachbrook 🦚

Along the A452, just north of its junction with the A41, lies the village of Bishops Tachbrook. The poet Walter Savage Landor lived here as a boy in the 1770s and his family are commemorated in the church.

St Chad's is 13th century with a Norman doorway and some blocked Norman windows. There are interesting monuments to the Wagstaffe family of the 17th century and also some William Morris stained glass.

The old village school was closed in 1962 and a new school built, which now has some 180 children. Many villagers have happy memories of the old building, which had only two rooms, heated spasmodically by large tortoise stoves filled with coke. They were either red hot or stone cold, there seemed to be no happy medium. Occasionally one or the other of them would belch forth clouds of thick yellow smoke, filling the whole building. All the children would be sent home – much to their delight!

Bourton-on-Dunsmore & Draycote

This parish which includes Draycote hamlet, is an ancient one mentioned in Domesday Book 1086 with a population of 150. Today it is around 300.

The parish lies on the southern part of Dunsmore Heath, sloping south to a valley in a tributary of the river Leam. Bourton village is on the higher level (107 metres above sea level) and Draycote in the lower valley (76 metres) – ¾ mile down the hill from the parish church. Although divided by geographical features and neatly separated by a now unused railway line, the two communities have much in common – Church, Parish Council, WI village hall and numerous other groups and activities.

For centuries the land provided the main employment. Before 1939 few men worked outside the parish, the rest were estate and farm workers living in tied houses. The farms remain but the many working horses have vanished, and the farm workers are few.

St Peter's church standing on the edge of the heath is early 13th century. It contains much of interest including a magnificent 13th century font, a parson/clerk pulpit dated 1607, Jacobean altar rails, and it is said, a very friendly ghost in the vestry.

Bourton Hall is a large stone mansion begun in 1791 probably on the site of an earlier house. The earliest recorded landowner was Lewin, a Saxon, who held the manor before the Norman Conquest. It remained with various branches of the family of John Shuckburgh who bought it in 1563, until 1906. Much altered and embellished by the new owner J. F. Shaw, it ceased to be a private home in 1947. After short spells of occupation by Jesuits and a Boys Preparatory School it fell into ruin. In 1979 Ingersoll Engineers bought it for their place of work and restored it to most of its former splendour – a good example of a near derelict house given a new lease of life, to the benefit of the company and the village.

The school was established as a Free School in 1836 for boys and girls, with the building and house attached built in 1847 by John Shuckburgh. It was closed in 1974. Now it, too, has been given a new use as a most attractive guest house.

Between them these three buildings once supplied a great deal of bell ringing. Estate workers for instance, were summoned daily to and from their labours by a bell in the private RC chapel at the Hall. No longer. Even in the church a chiming apparatus is now used. The bells, considered unsafe, were last rung, with some trepidation, for the victory of El Alamein in 1942.

The village hall is an extension of the 'Round House', which was actually octagonal and was probably a toll house with attractive curving architecture, once used as a laundry for the Hall.

One custom remains from earliest times. The parish annually on Martinmas Eve, before sunrise, pays its dues of 1½ pence to the Duke of Buccleuch, Lord of the Manor of Knightlow (Dunsmore is part of that ancient Hundred) at the ceremony of Wroth Silver on Knightlow Hill. If the parish defaults His Grace may demand the forfeiture of a white bull with red nose and ears of the same colour.

Draycote lies between hedgerows, trees, meadows and gardens alongside a brook. Belonging to the Lordship of Bourton, it was at one time in the ownership of the Dean and Chapter of Newark. The hamlet is still a peaceful, contained place.

For many years Draycote had a Baptist chapel. Dated 1811, it was rebuilt in 1869, closed in the late 1930s and is now privately owned. The preachers came on horseback or walked, from Coventry or Rugby. The site was reputed to have been previously occupied by a dance hall!

Draycote has given its name to a surprisingly large number of things: a former pottery; a cattery; transport; Draycote Water, the reservoir of whose 240 hectares 80 are in the parish; and the beautiful nature reserve, Draycote Meadows. Here are the flowers which Shakespeare would have known, 'Daisies pied, Ladysmocks and Cuckoo Buds'.

Brailes 🌿

The village of Brailes lies tucked snugly into the southernmost tip of Warwickshire, and is divided into two, Upper and Lower, straggling both sides of the curving main road running between Shipston-on-Stour and Banbury.

Brailes Hill, the second highest point in Warwickshire, rises soft and green towards the fringes of the Gloucestershire wolds, and is surmounted by a distinctive group of trees. The real name of this is Highwall Coppice, but to all Brailes locals it is simply Brailes Clump.

On the other side of the village street is the man-made mound of Castle Hill, a dome topped earthwork, once an ancient burial ground. At one time this was used as a base for a castle of the motte and bailey type, but no trace of it now remains. The walk across the fields and the climb to be 'King of the Castle' is a popular weekend pastime for Brailes' youngsters and their parents.

In medieval times Brailes was a thriving and bustling market town, the third largest in the county, and its former prosperity is reflected in the fine church of St George in Lower Brailes, referred to as the Cathedral of the Feldon. It has many points of interest and there are stones from the 11th century built into its 14th century walls. However, like many such churches it suffered somewhat at the hands of the Victorians.

Feldon is the name given to this rich area of fertile farming land, and aerial surveys have revealed traces of earlier roads and villages where now there are productive fields. Walk to the top of the hill, and look at the panorama below, and remains of the old ridge and furrow cultivation are very evident all around.

In addition to the fine parish church, the village is fortunate in its Catholic church of St Peter and St Paul, built in 1726 in the upper part of a barn adjoining a farm. It is so well hidden, in fact, that the casual visitor would have difficulty in finding it.

There is also a Methodist chapel, built in what was referred to as the 'Italianate' style in 1863.

A few notables have lived here, and not too many of the infamous. Perhaps the most famous son was William de Brailes, who was one of only two known English artists responsible for some of the beautiful and delicate work on illuminated 13th century manuscripts. His work has been exhibited at many specialist museums and art galleries, but can be seen on permanent view at the Fitzwilliam Museum, Cambridge. It is signed with his own 'portrait', a tiny, bent figure with a shaven head.

Another notable was the doctor who served this village for more than 34 years. Dr Findlay first came to Brailes in 1894. What was truly remarkable about Dr Findlay was that he was a keen amateur photographer in those early days when you had to get beneath a black cloth and photograph on to a black glass plate. Dr Findlay was always asking people he met on the road to 'hold still'. When he died in 1928, he left behind a most precious legacy in the form of a photographic record of Brailes.

The most infamous resident was undoubtedly Nance Austin, the Brailes witch, who lived alone, and had a familiar in the form of a cat. Her speciality was levitation. Recent restoration in Nance's old cottage wall brought forth the remains of an old chimney sacrifice and one of her ancient shoes!

Brinklow &

This is a village which goes back to pre Roman times as shown by the 'tump', thought to be an ancient burial mound. The village is noted today for its location on the Roman Fosse Way and on the popular modern holiday route south to the Cotswolds.

Visitors are encouraged to visit the 13th century church full of interesting features. On a fine day one would be rewarded by browsing in the churchyard, where an interesting headstone can be found to the memory of a deaf and dumb woodcutter, showing a bundle of faggots, a woodman's glove, an axe and gorse hook. Beneath is inscribed:

> This man his character to sum,
> From infancy was deaf and dumb,
> His understanding yet was clear,
> His heart was upright and sincere,
> He chiefly got his livelihood
> By faggoting and selling wood,
> Till death The Conqueror of all,
> Gave the feller himself a fall.

Over the centuries the great houses of Coombe Abbey, Newbold Revel and Town Thorns, when in full glory and entertaining many guests, employed many villagers. Basketweaving, candlemaking and the manufacture of silk took place in the village itself and the development of the canal and the railway added to the prosperity of the village.

As in all villages the school has always been at the centre of life. In past years absenteeism has sometimes caused problems. Children were drawn away by Lord Craven's shooting party or by the meet of the local hunt, and the procession of Barnum and Bailey's Circus in Coventry and Buffalo Bill's 'Wild West Show' in Rugby also created a problem for school attendance!

The Johnson family run the oldest surviving business in the village. For over 400 years they were wheelwrights, builders and undertakers and still practise the latter trade.

Broom ᘛᕐᘁ

Broom is a small village in the Parish of Bidford-on-Avon, not far from the Vale of Evesham. Having a population of just over 400 and 152 houses, it is a compact little village.

The buildings are a mixture of ancient and modern, some of them being 16th century. The earliest of these is said to be The Broom Tavern, which was built as a farmhouse. With its timber framing and red brick in-fill, this building when floodlit, makes an impressive sight. Another old building is The Broom Hall Inn, also built as a farmhouse and dated 1577.

Earlier than either of these is the Mill, said to have been started by the Monks of Worcester. There used to be two mills under one roof, and these were mentioned in the Domesday Book in 1086. Of course the building will have been repaired and has been greatly extended.

The Mill stands on the banks of the river Arrow, which flows gently past the western side of the village. The Arrow rises near Birmingham in the Licky Hills and after flowing down past Broom, joins the Avon about 2 miles downstream.

Before the bridge was built over the river in about 1900, the river had to be crossed by a ford near the Mill. One horse and cart got swept away in the current, when the water ran high. That first river bridge was finished just as a bad flood came, and it was washed away. Its replacement lasted until 1964, when a stronger bridge and wider road was needed to take so much traffic.

The railway came to Broom in 1866, when the Evesham to Redditch line was completed. This was a boon not only to Broom,

Sixteenth century Broom Hall Inn

but to the surrounding villages too, and was a great loss when it closed in 1962. Now, Broom Junction is a Council yard, and the old railway cuttings have become like nature reserves.

In Mill Lane stands the small church of St Matthew, with services twice each month. This was built in 1868.

Broom is one of the villages mentioned in the verse by William Shakespeare (see Temple Grafton). This is 'Beggarly Broom', though anyone walking round the village will find this hard to believe today.

Bulkington 🪶

The village of Bulkington lies to the north of Coventry in the Borough of Nuneaton and Bedworth. In the Domesday Book, Bulkington is called Bockintone and it seems likely that Anglo-Saxon settlers were attracted by the higher, well-drained land and the plentiful supply of water from the many springs, which abound to this day.

Farming is still an important economic activity in the countryside which surrounds Bulkington. By the time of the Enclosure Acts ribbon weaving had become the major occupation of the villagers. George Eliot knew Bulkington well and referred to it as Raveloe in her book of the cottage weaver, *Silas Marner*.

In 1801 the population was over 1,300, but the fact that there was no coal under Bulkington restricted industrial development and the village remained in a rural setting. Today there are over 9,000 inhabitants with the majority of the workers commuting to the surrounding towns and cities.

Christian worship was likely in Bulkington before the Norman Conquest. The parish church of St James dates from the 13th century, though documents prove that a church existed on the site in 1143. A fragment of this earlier church is incorporated in the modern porch. The 15th century tower houses a fine peal of bells, four of them being over 300 years old. The remaining four are modern. These are rung by an active team of bell-ringers.

In the church are several examples of the work of the amateur sculptor, Richard Hayward, who lived at the manor house Weston

Hall in the 18th century. A particularly fine piece is the font sculpted in Cararra marble, which stands upon a plinth bearing this inscription: 'This fragment of ancient Numidian marble was imported by Richard Hayward and given to this church MDCCLXXXIX'.

The box pews in the body of the church were placed there in 1821, and this event is recorded at the base of the tower. The pews bear the scars inflicted upon them by generations of Bulkington children bored by long sermons.

The churchyard is noted for its table tombs, and one which stands to the right of the porch is to the memory of Mr and Mrs Johnson, uncle and aunt of George Eliot whom she portrayed as Uncle and Aunt Pullet in her book *The Mill on the Floss*. Devotees of George Eliot travel to Bulkington from all over the world just to look at this tomb.

The manor house, Weston Hall, was built in the reign of Elizabeth I, by the De La Zouche family. Today the Hall is a hotel but retains the original Elizabethan facade. The stable-block, added in the late 19th century by Francis Newdegate, lord of the manor was restored in 1988 from a ruinous state to provide high-class dwellings.

The Borough Council has designated a part of the village as a Conservation Area and in the Ten-Year Development Plan no major housing or industrial building is to be allowed.

Burton Dassett ⟳

The parish of Burton Dassett is located in the south of the county close to the borders of Oxfordshire and Northamptonshire. It is made up of the villages of Northend, Knightcote, Temple Herdewyke and the smaller communities of Burton Dassett and Little Dassett.

Burton Dassett is the oldest part of the parish with its part Norman church, to be found just outside the area of the Dassett Hills, which is now a country park run by Warwickshire County Council. In years gone by this was a wild natural area with a post windmill at its summit, and also a stone beacon which is still there and visible for many miles around. 'Ghosts' seen on the hills have been put down to vapour rising from the natural springs there. In living memory stone was quarried there. A bridlepath, Mill Lane, leads up to the hills from Northend village.

Northend village is at the foot of the Dassett Hills and has a variety of old stone houses and also many modern properties. The first council houses were built in the 1930s. During the Second World War many evacuees came from Coventry and London and Land Army Girls from Birmingham. A small unit in the village made tools for munitions factories and the barrage balloon over Coventry was clearly visible from the Dassett Hills. Although the heavy bombing was very near at Coventry, the closest disaster was the crash of a 'Flying Fortress' bomber.

Midway between Northend and Knightcote is Granslet Pool with a paved base, where horses and carts were driven through for the wooden wheels of the carts to have a 'soak' and so not lose their iron rims.

Knightcote village has, over the years, lost its Royal Oak public house and school (both now residences). One row of thatched houses remains, however, the only thatched properties in the parish. Knightcote still has a post office/shop, village hall, Methodist chapel, and the farming includes a dairy herd as well as arable, sheep and cattle.

Just outside the village is Stockwell Spring – similar saline water to Leamington Spa water. Two brick and stone slab standpipe covers remain in the village – a reminder of the water supply from the Dassett Hills. This water still feeds cattle troughs on the Knightcote side of the hills and at least one resident collects water from here for a 'decent cup of tea'!

Temple Herdewyke is a new village (Army married quarters). The Army Camp site was agricultural land prior to the Second World War, and many older parishioners were employed on the farms and in the farmhouses there.

Within the parish boundaries there is an Anglo Saxon settlement and burial ground. At Little Dassett there was a Roman Catholic chapel – known now as Chapel Barn. The Battle of Edgehill was fought on the boundary of the parish in 1642 and the whole area is steeped in history.

Not much is known of John Kimbell who, over 500 years ago, left land for the benefit of the inhabitants of Northend and Knightcote. Locally it is understood he was down on his luck and was given food in Northend and shelter in Knightcote. This was obviously not forgotten and the children and senior citizens still benefit – albeit with cash instead of coal at Christmas, but every household still receives a loaf of bread at New Year.

Cherington & Stourton

Cherington House is an 18th century building which used to belong to the Dickens family, who had the picturesque habit of planting a chestnut tree to celebrate the birth of each new member of the family. As one Mrs Dickens had 13 children, they made an impressive row. Sadly they were chopped down in the Second World War.

Weston Park was once a handsome house which looked most impressive as villagers glimpsed it through the laurels as they journeyed to Shipston. When it was pulled down in 1934 the stone was used to build the former Banbury police station, while the furniture and pictures went to the United States.

Thatched cottages always look so attractive, yet they are not always comfortable to live with. Daddy Berrows was a real village character who lived in a thatched cottage attached to his shop, only one wall of which now remains. He had a lot of trouble with his thatch. First he spread tarpaulin over the top. Then when that proved inadequate, he stretched more tarpaulin underneath the thatch. Perhaps it is not surprising that he was never seen without his hat on, even indoors. Although he always had a huge, roaring fire in the hearth in the winter, the villagers said that the house never went up in flames because the thatch was too wet to catch fire!

Chesterton ✑

Chesterton is a very small hamlet, with a mostly 14th century church but no shop or pub. It is cut by the Fosse Way, and there are still signs of the Roman settlement. It used to have a large manor house on the hill behind the church, occupied by the Peyto family for centuries until 1802, when it was pulled down.

It was Sir Edward Peyto who built the windmill in 1632 and the watermill about the same time. The windmill is fully restored, and open to the public every two years. The watermill has still kept all the millworkings, but it is boarded up to protect it. Perhaps one day that too will be restored. The pond itself has been dredged out and is now used for trout fishing.

The threat of the M40 motorway now hangs over Chesterton.

Church Lawford & Kings Newnham ✑

The villages of Church Lawford and Kings Newnham are linked by an old sandstone bridge spanning the river Avon which separates them. Both villages have histories going back to the Roman occupation and before.

Church Lawford, recorded as Leileford in the Domesday Book lies off the A428 Rugby–Coventry road. The church, dedicated to St Peter, stands on high ground overlooking the Avon and was rebuilt in 1873/4 on the site where the 14th century church once stood.

Close to the church is Manor Farm with its beautiful timber framed Tudor house, one of the oldest buildings in the village. The Old Rectory and The White Lion are also interesting, especially the inn with its low beamed ceilings and panelled walls which are enhanced with brass hangings and ornaments, giving a warm and friendly welcome to visitors. Across the road from the inn is the Reading Room which was bequeathed to the village by the Townsend sisters over 100 years ago and is now administered by a Board of Trustees. The Room is well used by village organisations.

34

There are people in the village today who remember when there was a blacksmith's shop in Smithy Lane, with the smell of horses and hot metal and a smith who chased away the saucy children who sneaked into his shop to pump the bellows, by cracking a horse whip behind them.

After crossing the bridge to Kings Newnham, or Newnham Regis, as it used to be called, there are three ponds on the right-hand side of the lane. These ponds, or stews, were made for the monks of Kenilworth Abbey 1,000 years ago, where they kept stocks of fish to supplement their larders. Today the ponds are the home for a variety of water fowl and each year a pair of swans breeds there.

The Hall on the left of the road is a fine 18th century house, now a farm. In the grounds are two listed buildings, an ancient barn and the tower of St Laurence's church. The church was probably built by the Kenilworth monks, but the nave and chancel were destroyed in 1794. The bells were taken to St Mary's church, Monks Kirby, and the font taken to adorn the garden of The Hall.

Around 1850 Lord John Scott inherited the estate and one day after heavy rain, it was observed that water in the rick-yard, which had formerly been the churchyard, drained away remarkably quickly. After investigations near the old tower, a water-filled underground vault was discovered containing several lead lined coffins. One coffin contained the body of Lady Audry Leigh who died in 1640 and could not have been more than 17 years old. Plates on other coffins showed that they contained the bodies of Francis, Earl of Chichester, Lady Chichester, Lord Dunsmore and Sir John Anderson. However, the most interesting and intriguing coffin was unnamed and had in it the remains of a man who had been beheaded, the head being separately prepared for burial and laid with the body. Around the neck was a black silk ribbon embroidered with the initials T.B. This and the other bodies had been embalmed and covered with rosemary and other herbs, but once the coffins had been opened and the remains exposed to the air, they rapidly disintegrated.

Lord John Scott ordered the the coffins be resealed and replaced with a zinc cover over the vault and a brass tomb plate. The plate was later removed to protect it from vandalism and is now kept in The Hall.

At nearby Little Lawford (Lilleford in Domesday Book) used to stand Little Lawford Hall. Here in 1780 Sir Theodosius Boughton was murdered by his brother-in-law, Captain Donellan, who mixed poison with his medicine, hoping to inherit the estate, but instead was hanged at Warwick. Thus the male line of the Boughton's was ended.

Most of Little Lawford Hall was demolished about 1790 and the present building is early 19th century. This is thought to have been the stable block of the old hall which was reputed to be haunted by the ghost of one-handed Boughton, a forebear who lost an arm in the time of Queen Elizabeth I, and drives a ghostly coach and six across the grounds.

Churchover 🦢

Churchover is situated near the Warwickshire/Leicestershire border, north of Rugby, with less than 100 dwellings. It is set on a hill, overlooking the Swift valley, in pleasant pastoral land.

The church, dedicated to the Holy Trinity, was mostly restored in the late 19th century. It has a 15th century tower, a Norman font with a cover dated 1673 and two monuments from the 16th century. One of these commemorates the Dixwell family, who lived at Coton House, which is a mile from the village. John Dixwell (1607–1689) was one of the signatories to the death warrant of Charles I. At the restoration of the monarchy, he was forced to flee the country and became one of the founding fathers of Newhaven, Connecticut, New England.

A Manor House has stood on the Coton House site since Saxon times, but after the Norman Conquest it passed into the king's hands. In 1291 it was held in part by the monks of Coombe Abbey, who built a monastic grange. King Henry VIII granted the manor to the Duchess of Richmond and it passed, through various hands, to the Dixwells. In 1787 Abraham Grimes had a new house erected after a design by Samuel Wyatt. Francis Arkwright was the last lord of the manor and at the turn of the century Mr Arthur James became a tenant. Mrs Arthur James was godmother to

Queen Elizabeth the Queen Mother, and the oak screen at the entrance to the chancel in Churchover church was erected to the memory of Mrs James by Her Majesty.

In 1949, after the death of Mrs James, Coton House became an Apprentice Residence for the British Thomson-Houston Company (later AEI) and then in 1970 it was bought by the Post Office as a Management Training College.

Many years ago, the occupation of most of the inhabitants was agricultural, on the farms or as estate workers at Coton House. Later, when the engineering works came to Rugby, a large number went to work in the factories. The farms have now dwindled to two.

The village school was closed in 1973 and the children now travel to Monks Kirby and Rugby for their education. The building is now used as a Community Centre. The village shop, which had stood in the same place for probably about 100 years, has closed, together with the post office.

About ¼ mile outside the village, by the lane leading to the next parish of Harborough Magna, a North Sea Gas distribution installation was built in the early 1970s. Landscaping has helped to obscure the extensive pipework and valves, but it is still something of a blot on this very rural scene.

Claverdon 🖾

Claverdon, with a population of 1,245 in 1986, sits astride the B4095 Warwick to Redditch road, in the old Barlichway Hundred and Arden Forest. Mentioned in the Domesday Book as Clavendone, the Early English 'Claefer Dun' or Clover Hill, pronounced in living memory as 'Clardon', still has plenty of clover to be seen.

Claverdon can boast two features which are poles apart in their uniqueness. One is the much photographed forge, said to date from the 17th century, with a horseshoe shaped archway for which Mr Darwin Galton was responsible. Happily there is a farrier working there again. The other, to be found in the Church Centre, is an embroidered panel approximately 9 by 5 feet,

The seventeenth century forge at Claverdon

designed by an embroideress and executed by herself and eight friends who were all keen amateurs when they started. It depicts village life in 1980.

A very distant ancestor of the Princess of Wales (who was Lady Diana Spencer) has a magnificent monument in the church, which he had built for himself. He was Thomas Spencer, second son of Sir John Spencer of Althorp, born about 1547 and died at age 82 in 1629. It had been a wise move on his part to have a monument erected, as with no immediate family his kinsfolk did not bother to add the date of death to it. This same Thomas Spencer was probably responsible for building the Stone Manor, an unusual three storey structure about which there is much conjecture. Pevsner asserts that it is a defensive tower-house, rare in the Midlands.

While Thomas boasts a fine monument, his funeral cannot compare with that of the scientist and explorer, Sir Francis Galton, who, it was said, 'was the most illustrious person to be buried in the Church yard', in 1911. He was a cousin of Charles Darwin, father of eugenics, developed identification by fingerprints and an early work, *Meteorographica* (1863) contains the basis of modern weather charts.

Schooling, first mentioned in the Rate Book for 1733, continues today in the village, in a modern building opened in 1966 to replace the National School of 1847. Mr Enoch H. Belcher was appointed Headmaster in March 1876, straight from college. He stayed until he retired 43 years later and lived on in the village until his death. He was a true 'character'. He organised most of the clubs and activities in the village, formed a brass band, leading and conducting it and started the cricket club which still flourishes today. When the Parish Council held its first meeting in December 1894, he was elected as the first Chairman. For many years he was church organist, too!

The church, with dedication to St Michael and All Angels and sister parish at Preston Bagot, may not be outstanding architecturally and was much restored by the Victorians, but has a most calming and restorative atmosphere for all who cross its threshold.

Geologically interesting is Tattle Bank, an area of sandy gravel forming a capping to the underlying red clay of Keuper marl. The gravel was formed during the Ice Age some 250,000 years ago, when two great glaciers invaded this area, from north-west and north-east.

Clifton-upon-Dunsmore

The village of Clifton-upon-Dunsmore is situated some 2½ miles east of Rugby on the western slopes of a fairly steep hill which, at its highest point, is just over 400 feet. Near to the village is Dow Bridge at which the three counties of Warwickshire, Northamptonshire and Leicestershire meet. One and a half miles north of Clifton are the extensive remains of a great Roman military station called Tripontium.

The village is said to take its name from its location – 'Cliffe' in Saxon signifying rocky ground, and 'Dunsmore' on the top of a hill.

During the reign of Edward the Confessor (1042–1066) Clifton was in the possession of the Sheriff of Warwick, Alwinus Viceomes or Alwyn, founder of the Arden family. Alwyn gave his land at Clifton 'for the health of his soul' to the priory of St Michael's of Coventry, which had been founded by the Earl of Mercia, Earl Leofric husband of Lady Godiva. It is very likely that the monks of Coventry built a dwelling and chapel on the present site of the church.

As the population of Clifton village increased in the 14th century, so the church grew in size, the nave, south and north aisles being added in that century. It is probable that towards the close of the 14th century the church was rededicated to the glory of the Blessed Virgin Mary. It is now commonly called St Mary's.

The large squat tower was the last main part of the church to be built in the 16th century of sandstone. Originally it possessed a tall, tapering spire which is thought to have collapsed in a great storm and demolished several dwellings in what is now Church Street.

The tower has a west window above which used to be clearly visible a curious muzzled bear figure – the outline of it can still be seen. It is likely that the sculpture is the crest of an old influential village family called the Barfords, their crest being a bear sable.

There is an ancient couplet relating to the bear inscribed on the court roll of the Manor, giving a warning against the dissipated habits of the time:

'Ye yonge men of Cliftone
Of Ye Lyon Bewayre
If your wish to be happy
Turn in at Ye Bayre.'

The Lion Inn was one of two public houses in Clifton, the village hall now standing on its site. The couplet was advising men to turn into church rather than frequent The Lion. The other Clifton public house, The Bull Inn, once a Hanoverian farmhouse, is still thriving in Main Street. Legend tells of an underground passage leading from The Bull to the church – for what purpose one can only guess!

40

The population of Clifton rose swiftly in the 19th century. In 1841 it was 364 and 585 in 1881. There is evidence from the census records of a good deal of overcrowding and actual housing shortage during this period. The coming of the railway to Rugby in 1838 and the opening of the Clifton Mill experimental crossing in 1864 had a profound effect upon the village.

Coleshill ᥦᣠ

Coleshill dates back to Saxon times, but it gained in importance when it became a staging-post in coaching days along the main London to Holyhead route. At that time it boasted more than 20 inns.

The most notable feature is the handsome church, built on the site of one which existed in the time of Edward the Confessor. The font is a rare example of Norman sculpture. Set in the floor of the chancel is a brass figure of the first vicar of the Reformation, John Fenton. This is a 'must' for brass rubbers, because his right hand displays five fingers and a thumb.

Outside on Church Hill stand the stocks, unique in Warwickshire because they combine a whipping-post and a pillory.

Another landmark, the towers of the power-station, are called after Hams Hall, once the home of Lord Norton. Here the constitution of New Zealand, which paved the way for it to become a self-governing colony, was formulated in 1850.

Famous local people include Simon Digby, awarded the manor of Coleshill in 1496 by Henry VII after the battle of Bosworth, and his wife Alice, who established the first charity in the parish for poor children.

A more infamous character was one John Wynn, owner of a cinema on the site of the present Cameo Suite. He operated a transmitter in the roof of the building during the Second World War and was caught giving information to the Germans.

Stories abound of two ghosts, one of a lady who appears on the stairs in Queen Anne House in the High Street and one of a highwayman who is reputed to have hidden in the cellar of a cottage where now stands an estate agent's office, also in the High Street. He does not appear, but can be heard moving about in the building.

Strangest of all perhaps is the elephant that choked on a mangold and expired outside The Bell Inn on the Birmingham Road, and is buried under what is now the Sons of Rest bowling green.

Corley

At the start of the century a rector and his family, by the name of Hamilton, lived at Corley Rectory. In 1942, 40 years on, the Rector's son had a dream in which he relived his childhood days. So deep were his thoughts he felt compelled to put them into verse, and called it *Corley 1902*. This is what he wrote:

'For this is Corley Lane, I know by heart
That bend, that slope, driving the governess cart,
And Gipsy, stubborn pony, knows them too;
In each unchanging house I know who's who;
Here at her gate good kindly Mrs Wall
With the twisted smile will answer if I call;
Here wizened Pettifor lives, and Steeley there,
Silent, important man, the carrier,
Who from his high-wheeled cart looks grimly down
On the slow-motion road, full five miles long, to town'.

What a gem of rural England can be envisaged, and what a wealth of information is revealed. The motor car had not arrived, the horse held sway, and the knowing of who's who was a true picture of Corley in 1902.

Hall Farm, which George Eliot so wonderfully describes in her book *Adam Bede* was struck by disaster in the 1920s. The dreaded disease Foot and Mouth was confirmed, thus destroying a lifetime's work. Happily, and to the relief of people with stock, it was self-contained, and was the only attack in Warwickshire.

Thankfully the lovely Saxon church and Church School are well

42

preserved. In the 1980s the school was threatened with closure, but the villagers petitioned for its retention and won. The school is still open.

The rich sanded Corley Rocks, with its wealth of bracken and bramble, was a wonderful playground for children, who came in droves from nearby Coventry and Bedworth. The woods, too, were a big attraction, especially at bluebell time.

It was after the First World War that the carrier's slow-motion road became the route to the booming town of Coventry and began to draw people away.

In the 1950s came the motorway. How sad to see the changing face of part of the village. Gone for ever was the natural beauty of some of this familiar landscape.

Coughton ✍

The modern village of Coughton straddles the M435, Icknield Street, 2 miles north of the market town of Alcester. The bulk of the village lies to the west of the main road along Coughton Lane and Wike Lane and to the east along Millford Lane.

The ancient village, mentioned in the Domesday Book under the name Coctune, lay between the Forest of Arden and Feckenham Forest. In 1300 the whole village west of the river Arrow, a tributary of Shakespeare's Avon, was taken into Feckenham Forest by King John. Opposite the post office, surrounded by railings, are the remains of an ancient stone cross marking the end of Feckenham Forest. Travellers are said to have given thanks here for a safe passage through the Forest.

There are still several examples of ancient cottages, albeit much modernised. Some of the houses in the village are Georgian, some Victorian and the rest modern. Long before the Tudor village there was a Roman settlement called Wike or Wyke, hence Wike Lane.

The Manor House, Coughton Court, belonged to the Throckmorton family who gave it to the nation in 1945, but who retained the contents and a portion of the house as their residence. The present house dates from the beginning of the 16th century and was built either on the site of, or as an enlargement to an existing house. It is now a National Trust property and open to the public.

The parish church, next door to the Court, was built by Sir Robert Throckmorton between 1486 and 1518. It has a peal of 6 bells which were restored in 1976 and are still carried in their original wooden frame. The Roman Catholic church and presbytery lie at the southern end of the Court driveway and were built towards the end of the 19th century.

The thriving village school which serves the surrounding area, was originally housed in an ancient barn, now a residential home for the elderly, along the main road towards Studley. It was eventually moved to a purpose-built Victorian school house in Wike Lane. When this school became too small, the 'new' school, dating from the mid 1950s, was built in Coughton Lane and today both schools continue in use. Further up Wike Lane lies the old railway station built in 1868 and now enlarged as a private house called 'Booking Hall'.

The village is still fortunate enough to have a shop and post office, two churches, a bus service and a pub (although technically this is in the parish of Sambourne). The only thing missing from the last century is the railway.

Cubbington ༻

Cubbington was mentioned in the Domesday Book of 1086, the first spelling being Cubitone. The ancient spelling was Cobynton which was derived from 'town of the descendants of Coba'.

Prior to 1950 the village consisted mainly of small back-to-back cottages with gas lighting and in some cases paraffin lamps. Water was obtained from a pump or well, but in the main street of the village water was drawn from a spring. Communal wash-houses were used, these being allocated to the housewives on a certain day each week. Sewerage was not connected until after the Second World War.

Mr L. B. Thwaites formed his company on its present site in 1938, employing a few men. As Thwaites Limited, there are now over 200 employees, producing dumpers and small excavators which are exported all over the world. Two other local employers are the saw mills which have been in the village for about 100 years, and Stereomatic Limited who manufacture high precision components.

The two churches, Anglican and Methodist, have always played an important part in the village. At one time there was a lot of conflict between them but for several years now they have held united services. From 1792 to 1820, the vicar of St Mary's parish church was the Rev James Austen, the brother of Jane Austen, the famous novelist. During the period 1918–1952, the Rev P. T. Broadway was the vicar and he and his wife did a great deal for the church and the village. One of the roads in the village is named after him. On the north side of the chancel hangs the Abraham Murcott memorial. On the shield is painted 'Abra. Murcott Mariner 1702'. He is reported to have been lost at sea during a dreadful storm.

It is said that two local men going to a football match were involved in an argument and in the fight which followed, one had his earlobe bitten off. From then on, men of the village were nicknamed 'Cubbington Earbiters'.

There was great excitement in the village on a morning in early November 1605, as the sound of galloping horses had been heard in the middle of the night. The next morning the news broke that on 5th November 1605 after Guy Fawkes was discovered and seized at the Houses of Parliament, Robert Catesby and some of his conspirators had set off to meet their confederates at Dunchurch. From there Catesby and his followers made a wild dash by night for Wales, riding through Princethorpe, Weston-under-Wetherley and Cubbington to Warwick, where they stole horses from the castle.

During the Second World War the villagers opened their already over-crowded homes to evacuees from Coventry, Birmingham and London. Some of these evacuees have remained and made their homes in the village. Mr Horace Lloyd and his firemen crew were awarded the British Empire Medal for their work on the night of the Coventry Blitz, 14th November 1940.

Curdworth 🌿

The name Curdworth evolved from Credeword, 'Creda's Settlement'. The original settlement was a Saxon clearing in the Forest of Arden near the river Tame.

The parish church of St Nicholas dates from 1165 though there was probably a Saxon church on the same site before then. In 1895 Lord Norton restored the church at his own expense and Prime Minister Gladstone visited to view progress of the work. There are many interesting features: medieval wall paintings, a 13th century ten feet long dug-out chest, carved from a single tree trunk, and a 15th century silver bell, given by a traveller lost in the forest who was guided home by a bell tinkling in the church. In the floor of the nave is a memorial to Cornelius and Anne Ford, of nearby Dunton Hall. Their daughter Sarah was the 'dear honoured mother' of Dr Johnson.

The church is on rising ground, dominating the village, and is adjacent to a rectangular site which is possibly the site of a very early manor house. Below this is 'The Battlefield', a tree-lined hollow reputedly the scene of the first skirmish of the Civil War in 1642. Sir William Dugdale guided soldiers through the forest towards the king at Nottingham, taking arms and supplies. Parliamentarians pursued them and crossed the bridge over the Tame and a battle ensued near the church. The king's men supposedly won.

Curdworth has evolved from being a rural area, with agriculture and later the Severn Trent Drainage Board dominating the economy, to its present somewhat undefined status. There is now much less dependency on farming although quite a lot of flat, open land around the village is intensively farmed, producing wheat, barley and latterly, rape. With growing development the village has become a 'dormitory' for nearby Birmingham, especially since the advent of the M42 and access to the M5, but there is still a friendly village atmosphere and feeling of continuity with the past.

There are many charming old cottages. Three cottages at the corner of Farthing Lane were originally a timber-framed Tudor farmhouse and later a coaching-inn called The Royal Oak – the oakleaf motif is still above the large inglenook fireplace in the middle cottage. Although modernised, some interesting internal features have been retained. Two are owned by the Water Authority and the smallest is privately owned. Curdworth Hall Farm, about 300 years old, is built on a base of medieval sandstone. Some of its windows are of hand-blown glass and some iron-framed, with butterfly catches. There are large stables and this could have been a 'Bush House', or inn, for travellers using the old turnpike road. The small pond is believed to have been the fish pool for the original Curdworth Hall and the moat is clearly defined – probably a status symbol, rather than for defence! Another two cottages about 250 years old were occupied by the blacksmith and family and until 1975 there was an adjoining forge, now replaced by a modern house. It is thought that the Civil War skirmish was partly fought on the rear garden of these cottages.

Dosthill & Whateley 🌿

Before the Second World War, Dosthill was quite a small village consisting of a cluster of farms, old cottages, the vicarage and Norman chapel, grouped quite picturesquely around the church at the top of the hill, connected by the High Street to some rather depressing coal miners' houses at the lower end of the village. The High Street itself was a rather grand name for a straggle of diverse houses, including some old cottages, some short terraces, and a few detached houses built mainly during the 1930s.

The chief employment was either mining (the mines being situated away from the village), or clayworking, there being a proliferation of brickworks in the area due to the rich supply of clay which was readily available. In contrast, there is also a unique outcrop of volcanic rock, and this was quarried for many years, leaving behind a hole filled with water nearly 100 feet deep, which is now used for sub-aqua diving. Many of the older people still living in the village remember the aerial buckets transporting the stone from the quarry, across the main road to the stonecrusher which was sited at the brickworks.

The countryside to the west of the village is known as the Roundhills, a series of slopes levelling out into the valley of the river Tame. Being mainly unfit for cultivation it is ideal for rambles, and after winter snow, for tobogganing. The view from the highest point is magnificent, and the water meadows in the valley are extensive.

Since the Second World War a tremendous change has taken place, slowly at first with the building of a housing estate on farmland, but accelerating since the 1960s. Despite all these changes, Dosthill has somehow retained its village atmosphere.

All but two of the brickworks have disappeared, those remaining being tucked away and having no visual impact on the village. The old beehive kilns which had been allowed to crumble away, and the derelict land surrounding them, have been replaced by modern but attractive private housing estates, and the miners' houses have given way to comfortable accommodation for the elderly.

The oldest surviving building in the village is the Norman chapel, originally a chapel of ease, and used variously for church services before the present church was completed in 1872, and as a Dame School before the present school was built in 1887.

Other buildings of interest include a cruck barn belonging to Church Farm, and used until recently as a dancing school. Dosthill Hall, a Georgian house which was once a health spa, was allowed to fall into disrepair, but has been rescued and beautifully restored by its present owners. Mountside, a large late Georgian or early Victorian house, was built by the main landowner and one-time squire of the village, Mr Cheatle. The last survivor of this well-known family in the village was a maiden lady, Miss Maud Cheatle, who died in the 1960s. She was instrumental in the setting up of the local youth club, giving them land and money which has resulted in the club becoming probably the wealthiest in the country.

Whateley is just a hamlet atop an even higher hill than Dosthill, and just under 2 miles distant. Its old name was Wheatley, and for some years it was known by both names. In direct contrast to the larger village, it has shrunk rather than expanded.

The surrounding countryside has scarcely changed, there is no pub, church, or shop, and Whateley remains a pretty and peaceful, out-of-this-world spot, unspoilt and truly rural.

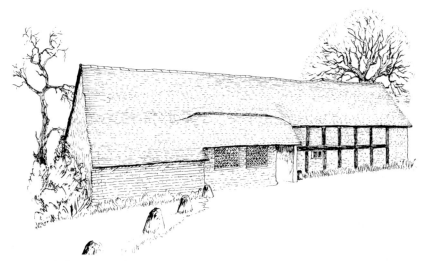

A cruck barn at Church Farm, Dosthill

Dunchurch

Dunchurch, or Don Cerce as it was known in 1086, stands on the old coach road from London and no doubt this is the reason for the 27 alehouses it once boasted! Now there are two, The Dun Cow, an old coaching inn and The Green Man public house. The inn where the Gunpowder Plot conspirators took refuge on their flight from justice is now a private house named Guy Fawkes House.

The old gaol, which was pulled down in 1972, once held overnight miscreants but the stocks on the village green are the only reminders of those days. The last person to be locked up was Peter Murcott who spent his night in gaol supping beer through a straw from a keg outside the window, probably left by his friends!

Standing at the crossroads is a magnificent statue commemorating Lord John Scott, once a local landowner. The statue was surrounded by iron railings which were taken for scrap metal during the Second World War. Each Christmas the statue is appropriately dressed by anonymous persons.

The Almshouses which were built in the 17th century have retained their old world look but have been fully modernised inside. Adjoining them are two private houses originally the boys school and the schoolmaster's house. The school for girls and infants was built in the churchyard in 1837. Some of the children came from very large families and started their education at three years of age. It is an interesting fact that when the school was demolished in 1929, the land reverted back to being the churchyard and so quite a number of people are buried literally where they went to school!

The parish church of St Peter, first mentioned in the Domesday Book of 1086, is still well attended and the many memorials in the church testify to the esteem in which it was held by previous inhabitants.

The village has always had a good supply of shops which catered for all the residents' needs. There are at least two dozen individual shops ranging from newsagents and grocers to designer clothes and shoes. One prominent local businessman's company developed a Formula One engine for the Williams motor racing team, including Nigel Mansell. Another local businessman owns Webster Wools and has numerous shops throughout the country. The Wool Shop in Dunchurch is open every day and is very popular.

Earlswood 🐾

Earlswood in the Forest of Arden has a romantic ring to it. The first known record of the name came in 1484 when King Richard III granted William Catesby 'an hundred oaks to be taken from the said King's old park of Tanworth or Earlswood in Tanworth within this county'. Only one house in Earlswood predates this: The Moat House, previously known as Cowernes, is a timber framed house dating from 1480 surrounded by a considerably older moat. It is thought that Richard Cowerne lived here in 1387 in an even earlier house protected by the same moat. The National Trust owns the house but it is not open to the public.

It was not until the commencement of building the Birmingham to Stratford-upon-Avon canal in 1783 by Josiah Clowes that Earlswood began to grow as a community. In 1813 plans were drawn up to build three reservoirs to feed the canal system. The Canal Company paid Tanworth Churchwardens £969.8.9d. for 51 acres of Earlswood Common and the reservoirs were completed in 1821.

These reservoirs, known locally as lakes, are the main feature of the area. The engine house built at the end of one lake dominates the landscape and still feeds the canal system with water. Commercial use of the canal ceased in 1936 but it is still in use for pleasure craft. In 1987 up-grading work ordered by the Government Inspector of Dams was carried out on the lakes, thus saving them for the future.

Early this century charabancs would arrive in Earlswood to disgorge their passengers for a 'day out' by the lakes. Cyclists would come in their hundreds. Local residents provided safe keeping for the bicycles for 2d. and many sold refreshments. Boats could be hired and fishermen lined the banks.

Today there is a flourishing sailing club formed in 1959, and fishermen still enjoy their sport.

Other activities very popular in the area are horse riding and golf. There is endless scope for walking and bird watching. Clowes Wood has been a nature reserve since 1974 and is part of a Site of Special Scientific Interest which includes New Fallings Coppice and the reservoirs. Birmingham Boys Clubs have a permanent camp site in New Fallings Coppice. Sadly some other woods in the area were lost when the M42 motorway was constructed.

The parish church of St Patrick was built in 1840 with money raised from the sale of land for the reservoirs and rebuilt in 1899. It is situated almost a mile from the centre of the village. A school was later built next to the church and most children travel here by bus.

The post office cum village store, a dress shop and hairdresser situated near The Reservoir Hotel form the nucleus of a very scattered village right on the edge of the county.

Most of the countryside is farmed and there is little industry, only a few small engineering units and a farmhouse cheese factory. There are still some houses without mains water or mains sewerage.

Easenhall

Tucked away in the north-eastern corner of Warwickshire lies the little village of Easenhall. About 40 houses cluster around an old pub and two farmsteads, one of which has a big 'listed' barn, with a high archway which gives access to the farmyard, and a 200 year old cedar tree. Some of the cottages and semi-detached Victorian houses used to accommodate the families of those working for the great house of Newbold Revel. In fact it is thought that the name Easenhall is derived from the fact that the village is near the eastern lodge of this estate.

Nowadays 'the Revel' is the major training college in the country for prison officers and the population of the village is made up of farmers, old established families and commuters who have been attracted by its unspoilt character and the fact that it is only 4 miles from Rugby and 7 from Coventry, with easy access to motorways, railways and airports.

The village has no post-office, shop, church or school but there is a former Congregational chapel which was sold to the residents some 20 years ago. This tiny building, consisting of one room with no facilities, has become the Village Hall. A good community spirit is also encouraged by participation in the County Best Kept Village competition, which the village has won several times.

The infrequent bus service and the telephone kiosk have been threatened from time to time but they have, up to now, survived. Easenhall is in the parish of All Saints, Harborough Magna which ministers to the spiritual life of the village and small children attend the Church of England First School there.

The Golden Lion is a popular meeting place for locals and tourists alike and retains its character of bygone days when it slaked the thirst of villagers with beer, perhaps brewed in the local brewery which is now a private house. The pub building dates from 1640 and still displays some of its wattle and daub wall.

The only home-grown legend is that of the Pailton Miser who lived in squalor in a tumbledown shack up Cord Lane, but was found, on his death in 1891, to be 'wearing' wads of £1 notes in his trousers!

One may catch a glimpse of the Phantom Horseman in the lanes at dead of night. He is the ghost of One-handed Boughton who died in Old Lawford Hall which was later burned down. In an attempt to exorcise his ghost, his remains were put into a phial and thrown into a nearby pond but – you never can tell!

Ettington 🌿

Ettington has grown up at the intersection of the two former turnpike roads – the north-south route from Warwick to Moreton-in-Marsh, and the east-west road between Stratford and Banbury. It was originally known as Upper Eatington, when Lower Eatington (once Etyndon, and 1½ miles away) was the main settlement. Here stood the fine old parish church, together with the mill on the river Stour, close by the manor house of the Shirley family. This village disappeared completely at the end of the 18th century when the Shirleys landscaped their estate, and by private Act of Parliament changed the old church into a family chapel.

They gave land for a new church dedicated to Thomas à Becket to be built on the hill at Upper Ettington which was now becoming the larger and more important centre. This church, opened in 1803, was built of poor local stone and only lasted for 100 years. The tower survives, as an interesting landmark, but the rest had to be dismantled and the present parish church, dedicated like the old one to the Holy Trinity, was built at the crossroads in 1903. The ruins of the old church in Ettington Park are well worth a visit for their historic interest and beauty.

The village also has a beautiful old Friends' Meeting House built in 1681, which is one of the oldest in the country to have been in continuous use. Ettington was a stronghold of Quakerism in the 17th and 18th centuries, and supporters of the Society of Friends suffered much persecution and hardship. There were also two non-conformist chapels – now converted into houses, and a Wesleyan chapel which has recently been demolished.

A few of the older cottages survive, especially around the Square which was once the hub of the village, but is now a quiet backwater hemmed in by newer houses, many built since the

Second World War, as the population has increased. Very few people are now employed in farming, though the village is surrounded by good arable land.

Though none of the Shirley family lives in Ettington now, the village is proud of its long connection with this family, which is thought to be the only one in England to have retained ownership of its estates through the male line from Saxon times. The name Saswalo is recorded in the Domesday Book and in the archives of Kenilworth Priory. The family house was handsomely rebuilt last century in the Victorian Gothic style and is now a prestigious luxury hotel. Change of use seems to have been the fate of many of the older buildings – the smithy, the bakery, the chapels, the toll house, the old school and the old school house (part of which was once the village lock-up), and more recently the butcher's and the greengrocer's, have all been converted into dwelling-houses. Even the old Thomas à Becket tower has been tackled.

There are two public houses – The Chequers and The White Horse – but The Saracen's Head on the old Halford road, and The Nelson Coffee House are both now private houses. The Saracen's Head took its name from the spring in Rookery Lane. Legend has it that a knight and his squire returning from the Crusades stopped by the spring to drink, and that their gory trophy – the head of a Saracen they had slain – fell into the spring and there fossilised, hence its inclusion on the Shirley family crest. The spring is said never to stop flowing even in times of drought, and at one time nearby cottagers obtained their water from it.

Exhall 🍃

From Ardens Grafton the road drops steeply to the north-west across the valley to the village of Exhall, with Oversley castle and Oversley woods on the opposing hills. The public footpaths around the village and over the hills are popular and frequently used by ramblers. In olden times the path from Exhall to Oversley was the main route taken by villagers having business or shopping in Alcester. Today this footpath links with the Heart of England Way, a long-distance walk stretching from Cannock Chase to Chipping Campden.

The village of Exhall

Exhall is recorded in the Domesday Book and its history probably goes back to Roman times (Roman coins have been found in
a garden in the village).

A local newspaper of 1939, in an article on the village, stated
that the entire working population was employed on the land.
Today only a tiny minority are so employed. The traditional farm
labourer has ceased to exist and over the past 30 years farm
labourers' cottages, as they became vacant, have been sold to
owner occupiers who have modernised and extended them, making them into very desirable residences for today's professional
and business people.

Village architecture is varied, reflecting the history and development of the village from Elizabethan to modern times. There are
some interesting black and white half-timbered buildings and one
farmhouse dating back to the 16th century. Most of the houses
stand on steep banks on each side of the road and this adds much
to the picturesque quality of the village.

The parish church of St Giles is unremarkable, having been
heavily restored in Victorian times. It is noted mainly for its fine
Norman door and the beautiful views from the churchyard.

There is a Parish Council which is actively concerned in preserving the village's peaceful and beautiful environment. The parish
boundary takes in part of the village of Ardens Grafton, as far as
the Golden Cross, the only public house within the parish and a
good 1½ miles from Exhall.

Local farmers, encouraged by government policy, are cutting
back on traditional farming and diversifying into new projects.
One farmer has made a motor-cycle scramble track stretching
from Rollswood to Grove Hill (the ridge of hills which separates
the Graftons from Exhall); another is converting farm buildings
into holiday homes. The orchards which were a feature of the
village in the inter-war years have now largely disappeared and
market gardening, once a significant occupation, has almost
ceased.

Farnborough

The village of Farnborough was originally called Fernberge or 'the little hill of ferns'. At the time of the Domesday Book the Bishop of Chester held most of the land. In 1322 it was sold to John de Rale, or Ralegh, a member of the Raleigh family of Devon. The Raleighs had financial difficulties especially after the Civil War and the Holbech family bought the estate in 1684 for £8,700. It remained an estate village until 1960 when it was transferred to the National Trust.

At one time the village was self-supporting with butcher, baker, basket makers and the women weaving at home. Most of the men worked on the farms and the estate. Farnborough Hall was double the size it is now and included a brewery and laundry. Until the Second World War, The Butchers Arms was only a beer house as the 'workers did not need anything stronger' and if spirits were required for medicinal purposes the Lady of the Manor would supply them.

Dame Berry lived in a house near the village pool in the early 1800s. One Saturday the foxhounds came to Farnborough and chased the fox into the village where it jumped onto the Dame's house and down the chimney. The old lady was very annoyed at this for she had just cleaned her house and the fox brought a lot of soot with him. She locked him in and when the huntsman came would not allow him to be taken unless they paid her a shilling. This was agreed and the fox was taken to Windmill Hill and liberated.

A thrush caught by the late Henry Holbech was buried beside the gravel walk at the Hall and the following lines marked his last resting place.

> 'Here lies the body of a poor thrush,
> Whom death unhappily did crush,
> Before he was fledged, young Henry caught him
> And to the cage he quickly brought him
> With care and tenderness he was fed
> And now alas! poor Dicky's dead.

And so must we frail mortals die,
And in the dust like Dicky lie.'

The parish church of St Botolph was begun in the 12th century
but has been added to over the years. A north transept and spire
added in 1875. There are memorials to some of the Raleigh family
and later ones to the Holbech family.

The church fete is called Farnborough Wake and is now held at
Farnborough Hall on the first Saturday in July. For many years it
was held on the Monday evening after Wake Sunday. If you
attended church on this day you were allowed to walk along the
Terrace Walk at the Hall. There is a 'Wake' pudding, something
like a rich bread pudding.

The village school is still going strong, with at the present time
57 pupils and three teachers.

There is still a very good village shop and pub, but the post
office closed some years ago. The village hall was built after the
First World War from an old army hut and still stands to provide a
place for meetings and the weekly whist drives and Christmas
bazaar.

Fenny Compton

Fenny Compton is set among the Dassett Hills, an attractive
village with many interesting buildings. The church of St Peter and
St Clare is one of only two churches in England with this dedication.

The name Fenny Compton means 'Settlement in a marshy
valley' and indeed it is the liquid assets of the village that bring it
temporary fame whenever there is a drought or a threatened water
strike. Such situations bring the Press and get the television
cameras rolling, for Fenny Compton boasts what is probably the
smallest Water Company in England, supplying just 40 consumers, ranging from large farms to the Village Hall, the bowling
green and private dwellings. The Water Company was formed in
1866 and financed by shares of £2 each. The Company office was
in the infants school room.

The water comes from one of seven springs in the Burton

Dassett hills from where it is piped to reservoir tanks and then to the consumers. The whole system is gravity fed. Over the years the Company has survived many problems and it is only due to the tenacity and loyalty of the villagers that it still exists today.

The quality of 'Fenny' water as it is affectionately called, has never been in doubt. It is the essential ingredient of a perfect cup of tea or home-made wine. It used to be that those who did not have their own supply would go to the stand pipes with their kettles, and visiting relatives would bring large containers in which to take the precious water home. To this day, people can be seen collecting the water from the overflow by the Avon Dassett road. One resident recalls that his father used to tell how he had been instructed, as a child, by the doctor to bathe his eyes daily in the water for medicinal purposes. It is certainly said to go well with a tot of whisky!

Of course, no one can foretell what the future may hold, but at the moment the Fenny Compton Water Company is paying its way. It is a piece of history existing in modern times, held in great affection by the village – long may it continue!

Fillongley

Fillongley is a neat, pleasant village in an extensive parish, situated 6 miles from Coventry, Nuneaton and Coleshill. It lies in a hollow, steeply bounded on the east and south by hills giving remarkable panoramic views.

There were once two castles at Fillongley, one being the seat of the powerful de Hastings family. Early records show that a portion of land known as 'Old Fillongley' was in the possession of the monks of Coventry at the time of the Norman Conquest. The most prominent building in the village centre is the 13th century church of St Mary and All Saints.

There are various charities in Fillongley which have their origins in the church: an educational charity, one providing gifts (now money) at Christmas for the aged and poor of the parish, and for many years a 'bread' charity which distributed bread to the needy.

An ancient custom was a market, held every Monday. Items offered for sale, such as eggs, butter, cloth, were placed on the steps of the Market Cross in the churchyard. Fees for the sale of these goods were collected by a steward and went to the Lord of the Manor. Fillongley also held an annual fair at one time, which commenced on the Eve of St John the Baptist and lasted for six days.

There is a curious tale of the huge tree, 'The Kinwalsey Elm', on the borders of Meriden, Fillongley and Hampton. It is known locally as 'Kinnesy Church', from the days when John Wesley and other divines preached beneath its spreading branches and its trunk was used for posting notices, as if it were a church door. The tale tells of a couple caught stealing from a hen-roost on a neighbouring farm. They were tried by a local jury, condemned and 'hung on the nearest tree'. Their bodies were cut down, carried to a nearby common, cast into a hole and a stake driven through them. It seems the stake was green and took root. It grew into a tree, with branches growing only out of its sides as its head had been blunted by the mallet.

The bustling village tradesmen are mostly gone now, the black-

The Bell Cottages, Fillongley

smiths, bakers, carpenters, painters, plumbers, shoemakers, wheelwrights, stone-masons, rope-makers, malters and weavers; leaving only names such as 'Weavers Arms', so called from the family of weavers who once lived there, to remind us of bygone days. Those who work locally now do so in the village shops or on the farms, others travel to the factories and offices in the nearby towns.

Fillongley is well looked after for 'refreshment'. It has four public houses and a Working Men's Club, formed in 1890. The village has a post office, hairdresser, newsagents (bed and breakfast), a well stocked general food store, a butcher's shop and a garage. It also has its own resident policeman.

Frankton ✑

Frankton formed part of the land granted by Earl Leofric to Coventry Priory on its foundation in 1043. After the Dissolution of the Monasteries this manor was kept in Crown hands until 1579–80 when it was granted to Thomas Thornton and Thomas Woodcock, from whom it passed to the Temple family. In 1680 Richard Temple sold the property to Sir Theophilus Biddulph of Westcoome, Greenwich, in which family it remained until after the Second World War.

The church of St Nicholas has a 13th century tower, but is mainly 19th century work. In the church burial register is the signature of Frederick Temple, 1821–1902, who was headmaster of Rugby School and later Archbishop of Canterbury. He attended a burial here of a member of the Powlett family.

The manor, built 1662, like most manor houses created its own fish pools and these are still in use during the fishing season. The first mention of the Rectory is 1304.

The old school just off the street was maintained from a charity paid twice a year: Lady Day and Michaelmas. In 1878 a 'New School' was erected and remained open until the early 1940s when the children went to Bourton Village School. The inhabitants of Frankton decided that what was needed was a Village Hall – so a Village Hall Committee was formed, and the school converted to a hall. The Village Hall is now rarely used and entertainment is held in the Friendly Inn.

Frankton is a quiet village. Most of the houses and bungalows are occupied by professional people.

Funds were collected at the end of the First World War for the erection of a 'Memorial to the Fallen'. The position of the Memorial was left to the mothers of the fallen – a wise decision. It is placed in the interior of the church.

Gaydon with Chadshunt

Gaydon is a small village with a population in the region of 300, just off the A41 more or less midway between Warwick and Banbury and some 12 miles from Stratford-upon-Avon. The spired church of St Giles was built about 1852 in a 14th century style to replace an old chapel and the clock is a war memorial.

The nearby hamlet of Chadshunt has its own church dating from 1312 and is being considered by the Church Commissioners for inclusion in the Redundant Churches Fund. For some years services have been held only during the summer, Harvest Festival being by candlelight. Unfortunately, due to the state of the belfry, the six bells have not been heard for many years. A very old iron clock mechanism was found in the bell tower in the 1950s during cleaning operations but no one has any knowledge of how it came to be there or that it was ever installed. It was cleaned and found to be in perfect working order.

Until the 1970s Chadshunt Hall had a magnificent herd of pedigree Hereford cattle and could boast of having won the Supreme Championship at the Royal Show.

Chadshunt was once more important than Gaydon but by 1879 the population of the two places reversed and Gaydon became the larger of the two.

Chadshunt can claim a connection with the battle of Edgehill in 1642, for near the boundary with Kineton there is a field known as Rupert's Headland. Here the Prince is said to have re-formed his cavalry after their famous charge. They had stopped to pillage the Parliamentary baggage left in Kineton but had retreated in disorder to this field on the unexpected arrival of Roundhead reinforcements.

The Gaydon Inn has been in existence for many hundreds of years. It was an important hostelry, being the only inn on the Warwick–Banbury road for many miles. In 1789 John Smith of Culworth, was caught in highway robbery on the Banbury Road at Gaydon and was locked up for the night in an upper room at the inn where he carved his name on a beam. He was taken to Warwick and tried at the Assizes and hanged that same year. The Malt Shovel is the other public house in Gaydon.

Farming has long been the main industry but like many areas, is now mostly arable. Some cattle, sheep and a few goats are kept. Some farmland has been sold for house building and the farmhouses have become private dwellings.

Several houses are built with Gaydon bricks made from the yellow clay found near the surface and drain pipes were made from the blue clay of the understrata. The brickyard became a County Council store and now a house stands on the site. The smithy is now a private museum of antiques mainly connected with agriculture.

Grandborough 🍃

The present name, Grandborough, can be traced back to about 1538. Other known variations have been Greneburgh, Raneberge, and Grendeburgh. It is thought that they all have the same meaning – Green Hill.

Set in the heart of unspoilt Warwickshire farmland, practically on the banks of the river Leam, Grandborough remains a quiet, peaceful haven. With the busy A45 and A426 roads being 2 miles away, there are few heavy lorries to disturb the tranquillity. Only the occasional rumble of farm machinery or at worst, the ear shattering noise of low flying RAF fighter aircraft on their training flights, disturb the atmosphere of serenity and calm.

It is a village with an assortment of cottages, houses and farm buildings. Many of the farm buildings are constructed in traditional Warwickshire red brick but these are now being interspersed by a number of more modern houses and bungalows.

As one approaches the village, three spires can be seen towering into the sky. One is the spire of St Peter's, the parish church, and the other two are those of Wellingtonian fir trees which seem bent on outdoing the original painting *The way to heaven*. The church was built of stone during the 14th century and villagers are frequently engaged in fund raising activities for renovation work both to the steeple and interior of the buildings.

Three hundred yards away from St Peter's lies the Primitive Methodist chapel built in 1856. It was here that a local preacher, Elijah Cadman, kicked the front panel out of the pulpit whilst preaching his sermon. To quote Cadman:

'I was telling the congregation that after the devil returned his last temptation Jesus ordered him off, and gave him a kick that sent him howling through the air. My foot being in harmony with my subject, gave a kick as to send the front panel of the pulpit flying down the aisle, whereupon some of the members shouted "Glory".'

There is a commemorative plaque set in the front panel of the pulpit and a framed manuscript relating the story.

Grandborough must once have been an important place as it boasted three inns. Only one, The Shoulder of Mutton, serves its original purpose, but The Harrow at Woolscott and The Royal George remain as tastefully modernised homes.

The village school, built in 1840, no longer exists as a school but as a house. Perhaps a little bit of the heart of the village went with its closure in 1974. Children now have to be transported to neighbouring villages but many of the locals can remember being taught in 'the little room' and 'the big room' from the age of four or five years until 11 or older, depending on the date of their school years. They look back fondly on the years spent there and many remember the motto which still remains as an inscription on an outer wall – 'Train up a child in the way he should go, and when he is old, he will not depart from it'.

One of Grandborough's claims to fame is that it was once connected with the famous 'Match' rugger balls. Mr Harry Timms (who still has relatives in the village) worked at Gilberts in Rugby

Grandborough Village

where they made the balls for many club and international matches. Even after his retirement he could be seen in his cottage doorway, stitching the balls and thus bringing world fame to Grandborough.

Great Alne & Kinwarton

Great Alne and Kinwarton, which straddle the B4089 Alcester to Henley Road, are not marked on some maps, but both have much to commend them.

The river Alne bounds the two parishes on the south-eastern side and gives its name to the village of Great Alne. It was known as the 'Alwine', meaning 'clear and bright' to the Britons who lived here and even now is a haven for wildlife. It also provides the power for Great Alne Mill, mentioned in the Domesday Book, which continues to grind wheat into flour.

Tucked under the hill on the outskirts of Great Alne is the Rockwell Standard factory, a reminder of the evacuation of many such factories from Coventry in 1942 into country areas. It stands on the site of Great Alne Hall and Park and brought considerable prosperity to the village, even if it was blamed for the few incendiary bombs which fell in the village during the Second World War.

A relatively small number of villagers today are natives. A few can tell how they saw the opening of the river bridge in 1912, accompanied by the distribution of buns and ginger beer for the children. Before that time, when conditions permitted, farm carts trundled through the ford, as they had done since Roman times, when there was a settlement here and soldiers from the garrison in Alcester guarded the crossing. Less than half a century ago, when the house known as Shawford was build on rising ground nearby, fragments of Roman pottery and a coin came to light.

Near the river too, at this point, in 1876 men brought the railway. A quaint engine known as the 'Coffee Pot', drew a few carriages back and forth between Alcester and Bearley daily until the end of the First World War. Usefully opened again for the Second World War, the line was finally closed when railways were nationalised.

The name of the only remaining hostelry, The Mother Huff Cap, which is believed to be found in no other place in the country, is explained in the following verse:

'Twixt Michaelmas and Martinmas
Old dame began to brew,
With half a pint of old malt
And half a pint of new.
First twenty gallons of Huff my Cap,
Then twenty gallons worse than that,
Then twenty gallons as amber clear,
And then she brewed the servants' beer.'

Kinwarton and Great Alne are indissolubly joined. The two charming churches have always been under one rector. The Memorial Hall, built in memory of those from both places who served in the two wars, is a meeting place for the usual organisations. The modern day school caters for children both of Great

Alne and Kinwarton, just as the old one did. This can be seen as one leaves Great Alne for Kinwarton. It was built in 1840 by the efforts of the rector, Richard Seymour, who was a frequent visitor. On the wall near the door is the ring to which he tied his horse.

Kinwarton has its special possession too. In a field near the church is a dovecote which in medieval times housed birds to augment the winter meat ration of the Lord of the Manor. There is only one other working model like this, and many visitors are attracted annually. The dovecote and the church are the only visible reminder of one of the 'lost villages of Warwickshire'.

Great Wolford

Great Wolford is the first village in Warwickshire, if you enter Warwickshire from the Four Shire Stone. This large pillar stands square at the end of the lane leading to the village, and once marked the ancient boundaries of Oxfordshire, Gloucestershire, Worcestershire and Warwickshire. Years ago illegal fights and bear baiting were held there – when the law arrived from one county, everyone just moved a few yards into another.

Great Wolford, with its small village green and attractive Cotswold style houses, many with gables and diamond patterned windows, has a cosy, compact feel and still retains a rural peacefulness that is often lost in villages today. The similarity of many of the houses is noticeable, due to the fact that Great Wolford was part of the estate of Lord Redesdale of Batsford Park until 1924 when it was sold.

It is still a farming village. There are no shops in the village now, but there is still a post office, which used also to be the village grocer, and a lovely Cotswold pub, The Fox and Hounds, one of the oldest buildings in the village. Some say it is 13th century, though some of its ambience is missing since all the lovely old tiles were taken off the roof and replaced with harsh new grey ones.

There is a thriving church which was rebuilt in the 19th century on the foundations of its 12th century predecessor. Not a beautiful church some say, but with one of the best views in Warwickshire across the valley to Little Wolford and beyond – a lovely place to rest. Sadly gone is the blacksmith's forge and the village school, but the buildings remain still.

Village life in the past, however, was very different from today, for there were many more children, and very large families would live in the two-up-two-down tied cottages, which are now modernised, extended and picturesque properties. Those who lost their jobs in the past, lost their homes and there was always the fear of the workhouse at Chipping Norton where they earned their keep by breaking stones for the road.

> When I was young and in my prime
> I broke my stones by half-past nine
> But now I'm old and getting grey
> It takes me all the blooming day.

Mostly the reminiscences are of happier times, playing endlessly in the fields and enjoying and relying on folk laws and country sayings to predict the weather, for instance

> When Cadly Clump wears its cap
> Wolford chaps will have a drap.

Great Wolford has expanded slowly – a little infilling here and there, but so far the village keeps its rural charm. Meanwhile the countryside changes little – the bluebells still bloom every spring in Wolford Woods and the snowdrops cover the churchyard as they have done for hundreds of years.

Grendon & Baddesley Ensor

Turn off the A5 between Atherstone and Tamworth and you are going back in time, for this is the old turnpike road from Watling Street to Coleshill, where until recently the toll houses still stood. The road is rather steep, and at the top you have views over four counties. On one side is Grendon, on the other, Baddesley Ensor.

Both villages are mentioned in Domesday Book. Baddesley was called Bedeslei, meaning that there was a church or chapel there in the charge of a bede or hermit priest. Grendon's land was given to Henry Ferrers by William the Conqueror.

In 1848 Baddesley's ancient church was pulled down and its old pulpit bought by the Wesleyan Methodists and installed in their chapel. This five-sided black pulpit is claimed to be the one from which the Protestant Bishop Latimer preached nearly 400 years ago. The same bishop was burned at the stake by Mary Tudor, saying: 'This day, by God's grace, we have lit a candle in England that shall never be put out.'

Baddesley seems to have a rebel tradition. In 1669 Quakers were considered rebels and their assemblies declared illegal, but they had a meeting house in Baddesley at an old manor house given to George Fox by his friend, Nathanial Newton. In 1772, when they were given freedom to worship, Baddesley Quakers built a meeting house of their own. The Quakers used the building until a hundred years ago, when it was rented to the Wesleyan Methodists. Up to 1931 Quakers from many parts of the Midlands made a yearly pilgrimage to Baddesley.

Meanwhile Grendon, not to be outdone by its neighbour's claims to original happenings, once boasted its own mint, owned by Sir George Chetwynd of Grendon Hall. The Chetwynd family was connected with the village for hundreds of years, and had inside the church a chantry chapel, one of the few in England to have its own fireplace. This ancient church of All Saints, whose first recorded rector was Henry de Grendon in 1253, has many interesting features.

It was Sir George Chetwynd who was enamoured of Lillie Langtry, the famous 'Jersey Lily', and who took part in a fist-fight with Lord Lonsdale for her favours. Sir George had a very extravagant life-style, he spent a lot of time at race meetings and entertained the Prince of Wales, with the result that Grendon Hall had to be sold, and was pulled down in 1933.

The villages today look peaceful little places, with all their history behind them. But appearances are deceptive. Baddesley recently had a battle to keep its Common, while now the villages are joining to fight a plan to start opencast coalmining in the area. The rebel tradition lives on.

Halford 🌿

If you drive carefully along the Fosse Way through Halford you may see Reg pushing his beautiful little truck REG 1. He will be walking to the bowling green carrying on a tradition of its care spanning over two hundred years.

The whole character of Halford Bowling Club has drastically altered over the years. Two hundred years ago the members were men of substance. Names recorded about that time are very familiar today. The descendants of Holbech, West, Verney, Shirley and Leigh still live on the ancestral estates. Fiennes Sanderson Miller Esq of Radway was one of the select band who met together one afternoon a week. This gentleman was the son of the famous architect who was responsible for many beautiful buildings in the Midlands. We can imagine them travelling on horseback, or maybe by carriage, from as far afield as Stoneleigh and Farnborough, those from the north having to stop as they entered the village in order to pay their toll. Others would have crossed the historic stone bridge where the Cavaliers won a victory in the Civil War. Now the players still come from other villages but are drawn from all walks of life, able to play only at weekends and during the summer evenings.

But did those eminent gentlemen really come for the sport? Or was it rather for the excellent venison from the parks of Charlecote, Ettington or Alscot, washed down with a good port, that was the attraction?

'Observe always that everything is the result of a change', said Marcus Aurelius Antoninus. Thus the solid stone built village hall has resulted from the demise of the school. Attractive dwellings have appeared which once were derelict cottages. The beloved cobbler's shop, a good meeting place, has gone, but Halford boasts a smart freezer centre. The picturesque, though dilapidated thatched building, a well known landmark, has been sacrificed to make the road wider. A new bridge has been built.

And what of the Bowling Club? The old Club House with its cellar below and cockpit above is no more, replaced by a smart new pavilion beside the green from which you may now see Reg emerging, having completed his work, enabling still, though changed, the continuation of the game mentioned by Ferrars of Baddesley Clinton who, in 1575, commented on 'The Great Bowling at Hawford'.

Hampton Lucy & Charlecote ⁕

Hampton Lucy and Charlecote lie half a mile apart on opposite sides of the Avon. They were once linked by a ford, now by bridges. Hampton Lucy is on the north of the Avon where the river makes a great loop on its way to Stratford-upon-Avon. On this side was the Forest of Arden. Charlecote is on the flat Felden south side where fertile land stretches to the Vale of the Red Horse and the Edgehills.

The lane between the villages runs alongside Charlecote Park, home of some of the most photographed deer in England; past Charlecote Water Mill, now working again after a lapse of many years and often open to the public; and over one of the earliest iron bridges in the country.

On the north-east edge of Hampton Lucy is Hampton Wood, an area of ancient woodland now in the care of the Warwickshire Nature Conservation Trust. This once formed part of the Fulbrook Castle domains purchased by Sir Thomas Lucy, who had inherited the Charlecote Estate in 1605. This Sir Thomas (the third) was said to be a friend of William Shakespeare. It was his grandfather whose deer the young Shakespeare is alleged to have poached! In the wood are earthworks, probably part of the boundary of the Lucy deer park. Hampton Wood has an Open Day in May when the spring flowers are at their most beautiful.

Since the 16th century, both villages have been bound up with the story of the Lucy family of Charlecote. The older houses, one in Charlecote and several in Hampton Lucy, are still thatched and were once Lucy estate cottages. Many were built in the local brick, the clay for which came from Brick Kiln Field near the mill. The first village schools were provided by the Lucys.

Both churches were rebuilt in the 19th century by members of the Lucy family. St Leonard's, Charlecote, rebuilt by Mrs Mary

Elizabeth Lucy in memory of her husband, stands within the parkland of Charlecote House and contains several old Lucy tombs as well as more recent family memorials. St Peter ad Vincula, rebuilt by the first Rev John Lucy, Rector of Hampton Lucy, is one of the earliest examples of Victorian Gothic and, when seen from across the river and fields, shows clearly in its architecture the inspiration of Worcester Cathedral. From the time of King Offa to the reign of Mary Tudor the parish had belonged to the See of Worcester and was called Bishops Hampton.

Beyond the church the house called Avonside was once Hampton Lucy Grammar School which numbered among its pupils Charles Maries, the eminent Victorian botanist. Many of the Maries family are buried in the churchyard.

Charlecote House is one of the most popular National Trust properties and part of any Shakespearean pilgrimage. Almost opposite its gates is a 'tumbledown' stile also part of local history. On the Hampton Lucy side of the river a footpath leads from Sal's grave – the burial place of a local witch – towards Stratford-upon-Avon along high ground above the Avon reputed to be 'The bank whereon the wild thyme blows' (*A Midsummer Night's Dream*).

This lovely part of Warwickshire is full of natural beauty, history and legend, and must have brought pleasure to millions – though living on a tourist route has its disadvantages, when visitors ignore speed limits or park on blind corners! However, it is in a vulnerable position, liable to damage from insensitive development and if the river were to be opened up to motor-boats and commercialisation, this tranquil stretch of Shakespeare's Avon with its swans and its willows, its yellow water lilies and its purple loosestrife would be lost forever.

Hampton on the Hill, Hampton Magna & Budbrooke 🌿

On 18th August 1642, before civil war became official with the raising of the Royalist Standard at Nottingham, an encounter between Parliamentarian and Royalist forces took place near Warwick. This was at Grove Park, Hampton on the Hill, the home of the Catholic Royalist, Robert Dormer, 1st Earl of Caernarvon.

The Dormer family built the Roman Catholic church at Hampton on the Hill, called St Charles of Borremo, after an Archbishop of Milan. It was completed in 1819 and was a gift to the parish. The tribune and crypt are reserved for the Dormer family for all time. The statue of Mary wearing a cross and chain is thought to be the only one in England. It denotes her appearance at La Salette, South of France, at the time the church was built.

In a block of houses at the entrance to Grove Park is a building which used to be the Roman Catholic school; the cross and the shape of the windows can still be seen at the gable end. The Church of England school used to be in Old School Lane, just below the Village Hall, (this has now been made into two separate homes). The Roman Catholic school closed in 1889 whilst the Church of England school moved from its original site to larger premises in the centre of the village. This closed in 1968 when the new school at Hampton Magna opened. For a short time the old school was an outpost of Warwick library, but this has been demolished and three houses have taken its place.

St Michael's, Budbrooke, which can trace an unbroken line of Incumbents and Vicars from 1273, was for many years the garrison church for the Royal Warwickshire Regiment, as their barracks were at Budbrooke.

The lectern in the church was presented by the 3rd Battalion and the Bible in the childrens corner was given by the Officers Mess. The Regimental Colour, an antelope on a blue background, hangs high on the north wall close to the parish War Memorial tablet. When the Regiment finally left Budbrooke Barracks, they made another presentation to the church, this time a weather vane.

The Barracks were slowly run down and the men moved to Glen Parva in 1960. Buildings were completely dismantled and finally knocked down to make way for Hampton Magna. Ash House stands between the last row of houses built for use by Army personnel and the first of the new houses at Hampton Magna.

Keeping the links with the Regiment, the pub, once called Bout Time, was changed a few years ago, to Montgomery of Alamein. Six flourishing shops, a school taking children from 5 years to 12 years and a thriving Community Centre all make up this 20th century village, with its roots firmly in the past.

Harborough Magna

This village in the Borough of Rugby, with its hamlets of Harborough Parva and Cathiron, has a population of about 420. It was mentioned in the Domesday Book, as having a priest and a mill.

The village was once self sufficient, with its own smithy, wheelwright and shops. There was work for men on the farms, but the largest source of employment, was at the timber yards, owned by William Ivens. The saw mills were at Cathiron, near the canal. Here the seasoned timber was put on to barges for its journey to the factories.

Carts and massive cart horses were kept in fields and stables at Harborough Parva. The men would take their teams of horses to collect the trees from the estates. These were loaded on the carts, and secured by chains. The horses would pull the trees to Rugby station, where they were cut into smaller pieces by a huge machine, and taken to the saw mills. If the estates were too far away, the trees would be loaded on to special trains, and taken to Rugby. One tree from the Lawford Grange estate, was so big, it needed 18 horses to pull it.

Pleasure boats use the canal now, watched by fishermen. There are pleasant walks around the lanes, and these are popular for horse riding. Farming is now the main industry, there are herds of Friesian and Jersey diary cows. Sheep, pigs, and goats are reared, also geese and free range hens.

There are many old houses. One built in the 17th century still has a wall of wattle and daub. The Old Lion originally The Golden Lion, built in the 18th century, is being restored after having a disastrous fire in July 1986.

St Mary's Nursing Home, was a maternity hospital from 1949–1983. This closed down, when the new maternity unit was opened at St Cross Hospital, Rugby. St Mary's was built originally as an isolation hospital. In the early years, before they used a motorised ambulance, a farmer would harness his horse to an ambulance and, taking a nurse with him, would set off to collect any patients for admission.

Harborough Magna C of E first school, is in the centre of the village. It was built in 1845 as a National School.

All Saints church stands on higher ground and has a list of incumbents dating from 1305. The clock face in the tower was replaced in 1983. The new one has an unusual design, showing the symbols of the four Evangelists.

Harbury 🐝

History in Harbury reaches back to before recorded time.

In the old quarries skeletons of plesiosaurus and marine dinosaurs have been found, over 100,000 years old, while Bronze Age cooking pots are the earliest proof of human habitation. By 500 BC the Iron Age chief Hereburgh ruled her tribe in a 'byrig' or camp, fortified by an extensive earthwork which still exists within the bounds of present day Harbury, whose modern name is a modification of the redoubtable lady's own.

The Roman Fosse Way marks one of the village boundaries and today one of the culverts the Romans built still carries away flood water in parts of the village.

The Saxons left proof of their presence in the ridge and furrow in the fields around, a recognisable result of their farming methods. Much later land was owned by the Knights Templars and is now remembered as Temple End.

Harbury is now a large village pulsating with activity and thoroughly forward looking. And yet the past has a strange way of reappearing. The Roman legions are still seen marching along the nearby Fosse Way, heading towards their ancient posting station under the hill. Men and horses are picked up in the headlights, only to dissolve as the car reaches them.

Behind the Norman church stands the old Wagstaff School founded in 1611. There, a ghostly figure in a black coat has been seen to hurry across the road and into the nearby churchyard, where he strides angrily round the church, and into the old school. Some say he was protesting against misuse of funds for the school. Others say that he only appeared when he did not approve of the headmaster. Someone even took a pot at him, and the bullet holes are still to be seen in the schoolhouse door. With the modern school at the far end of the village, he is now, presumably, out of a job. No one seems to know exactly who he was. But perhaps he lived in the cottage opposite. Certainly it has an eerie atmosphere with too many unexplained noises and objects which move themselves around, and sometimes disappear. No one ever chooses to live there for very long.

Hartshill 🌿

There is evidence of the development of the village of Hartshill for hundreds of years, since before the arrival of the Roman conquerors. It stands on an island of ancient rock off the range of hills overlooking the Leicestershire plains. For that reason it has attracted settlers ever since the Ice Age ended over the Midlands. The name Hardreshulle, now Hartshill, was derived from the Saxon words Heardred's Hill. Today several new housing estates have joined the village to the outer suburbs of Nuneaton and so it is hard to visualise the village of days gone by.

The poet Michael Drayton's cottage at Hartshill Green

Travellers may notice the bus shelter on Hartshill Green which is the local memorial to the famous poet Michael Drayton who was born in Chapel Cottage in 1563. Older villagers can remember the ruins of his small thatched cottage on this Green. Through the efforts of a present-day local poet, John Sherwood, the memorial bus shelter was built in the shape of a scroll from local stone donated by the quarry owners. Sir John Betjeman came to Hartshill to dedicate the memorial and quoted lines from Michael Drayton's poem *A Fine Day*:

> 'Clear had the day been from the dawn
> All chequered was the sky
> Thin clouds like scarfs of cobweb lawn
> Veiled heaven's most glorious eye.'

Oldbury Grange is an interesting country mansion built around 1904 by Mr Garside Phillips, the first manager of Ansley Colliery, for his son Joseph. Joseph later became 'The Boss' at this pit and his family the leading gentry in the village. His grandson grew up to become Captain Mark Phillips, a renowned horseman winning the highest award at Badminton and the hand of the Princess Royal, then Princess Anne.

According to local legend there are one or two ghosts wandering around the village. The favourite is the Nun or The White Lady who is said to wander in Oldbury Road or Coppice Lane as it was first called, and over the Oldbury Hills. Her presence probably arises from the fact that before the Norman Conquest a small nunnery was built at Oldbury as an outpost of Polesworth Abbey. The nuns kept bees and their hives were protected from the winds by specially built niches in a small facing wall. Until a few years ago there were always colonies of wild bees living in the thick walls of Oldbury Hall Gardens.

Haselor 🌿

Haselor has been a village from at least Saxon times, being mentioned as Haselove (a hazel bank) in Domesday Book and as having two Manors, Haselor and Upton. Haselor has a church,

12th century, half way between the two Manors, built on a hill that overlooks the countryside all round.

The Black Death visited the village in 1349 and a great many folk died, including possibly three rectors. There is a strong body of opinion that the original village was built around the church but that the villagers moved into the present part of the village to get away from the plague. There is still the base of a preaching cross just outside the churchyard.

The oldest house is probably in Walcote and is built on the cruck construction method. Haselor has a water mill (Hoo Mill) which ground corn for the Manor and is still used to press apples to make cider. The earliest reference to it is in 1559. Another cider mill can be found on display in Walcote.

The stocks in the middle of the village were last used in 1841 when boys who had trampled down a field of corn were punished. Haselor once had a workhouse which was turned into five cottages, now being one house called Little Manor. This stands by the old Village Green.

Cornelius Griffin (1846–67) was Haselor's most notorious vicar. He spent all his money on litigation, lived in the church to avoid arrest, but eventually ended up in Warwick Prison. There is a memorial to him and his sisters in the church.

An elm tree fell across the post office in 1916. It crashed through the thatched roof into the bedrooms. Amazingly the family only suffered scratches. The thatch was replaced by galvanised iron which is still there today. Only one person at a time can be served in the post office – it must be one of the smallest around.

Haselor once boasted a round cottage called The Beehive which housed a very large family with only one up and one down. Now all the old cottages have been modernised and are hard to recognise. The village pub has changed into private residences and farm buildings have been changed likewise. One of them has the old toll-gate posts as an entrance, a reminder that Haselor once had two toll gates, one at either end of the village on the main road.

Hurley ✑

Hurley is situated 11 miles north-east of Birmingham and its name means 'a clearing in the forest' – in this case, the Forest of Arden. It is an agricultural and mining village, population 2,000, with a growing number of commuters, especially since the M42 motorway opened nearby in 1986. Situated on a hill over 300 feet above sea level, there are extensive views all round.

Hurley church, situated at the top of the hill, is a small wooden structure, erected about 1860 for a Dame School, to be used once a week for a church service. In 1895 a brick school was built in the playground and the wooden building became a full-time church. In the mid 1950s more school buildings were erected to accommodate the children of mining families, brought into the village to work at the newly sunk Daw Mill mine and other local mines. The new school buildings were erected on the site of St Edmund's chapel which had long since disappeared. The cross can still be seen in the churchyard along Heanley Lane.

Atherstone House, late 17th century, is brick with stone quoins. It is said that, during Cromwell's time a cannon ball went down the chimney. Until recently the cannon ball could be seen in the garden. An early Georgian moated house, Hurley Hall, once housed a magistrates court.

The Holly Bush Inn, which used to have steps up to its front door, overlooked the Bull Ring where the village stocks were sited. Opposite The Holly Bush were some very old cottages with wattle and daub walls and dormer windows. One of these was called the Nutshell and, although very tiny, was the home of a very large family. On the right, going down Knowle Hill, was the blacksmith's forge. It is now a garage.

Dexter colliery was sunk on the south side of the village in the mid 1920s. It was demolished in 1987. The coal from Dexter was taken along a specially constructed overground track to Kingsbury colliery to be screened, and no spoil was allowed to be tipped on Dexter colliery site. This track has also gone.

On the outskirts of the village, where a brook flows through a spinney to the river Tame at Kingsbury, is the site of an old paper mill.

Hurley Common is a small hamlet one mile north of Hurley village. It has 30 or so houses and two public houses, The White Hart and The Anchor. Hurley and Hurley Common are well served by shops, clubs and public houses. There are a dozen or so farms surrounding the village and several small light industries.

The villages surrounding Hurley have many interesting features. Baxterley has a lovely stone church with a rare 12th century wooden crozier head, the oldest piece of church equipment in Warwickshire. The churchyard is ablaze with wild daffodils in the spring. Merevale church has many interesting antiquities. Merevale Hall and Merevale Abbey are occasionally on view to the public. Bentley has an interesting public house called The Horse and Jockey which, other than electricity, has never been modernised. Its sign shows the present Sir William Dugdale jumping a fence in the Grand National in the 1950s.

Ilmington

Ilmington, a village of approximately 600 inhabitants, bordering the Cotswolds and lying on the edge of a fertile farming valley, derives its name from 'the elm grown hill'. Evidence of the earliest settlers is thought to date from around 2500 BC.

Six farms provide limited employment but most people commute to nearby towns.

The first Christmas broadcast by George V, in 1934, was introduced by Walton Handy, the village shepherd and relayed to the world from Ilmington Manor, a fine Elizabethan house, once owned by the De Montford family. There are many old houses built from stone quarried in the parish until the 1920s. Crab Mill, an attractive house, was earlier this century the home of Lady Borwick (of Borwick Baking Powder), who was the benefactress of the maternity ward at the Ellen Badger Hospital, at Shipston. Professor Dorothy Hodgkin, a 1964 Nobel Prize Winner (the first woman since Florence Nightingale) now lives at Crab Mill.

E. P. Wilson, jockey and trainer of the Grand National winner in 1884 and 85, lived in Ilmington and trained horses over the downs, where nearby is a Roman burial ground and a clearly visible Roman road, said to have been a pig drovers route through to Wales.

There are two public houses in the village – The Red Lion, where the Court Baron met prior to Land Enclosure and The Howard Arms. The seat of the famous Howard family is at Foxcote, a nearby hamlet.

Ilmington has a chalybeate spring which was for many years renowned for its medicinal powers. Another famous watering place, Wells Close, had its own little house in the fields, where people could stay to take the waters.

The remains of a tramway, once the main form of transport to the village, can still be seen.

The church retains its fine Norman arches and the Roman Catholic church was used as a school until 1931. The Methodist chapel is used for weekly worship.

Ilmington still has a general store, post office, school, hurdle-maker, and orchards, but sadly has lost its blacksmith, baker and other craftsmen. The greatest change has been the conversion of the beautiful old stone barns into dwelling-houses.

Kenilworth 🦢

Although the number of houses in Kenilworth has increased during the past few years, the pleasant atmosphere of a community which is in close proximity to city, country and university still exists. Visitors come to enjoy glimpses of history mingled with good shopping areas and leisure facilities.

Kenilworth's history can be studied through the church of St Nicholas which has a beautiful Norman doorway which was originally part of the Abbey; the monastic ruins in the Abbey Fields, including the small museum open in the Abbey Barn on summer Sunday afternoons; and the castle, founded about 1120 and eventually destroyed by Oliver Cromwell.

In 1266 Kenilworth Castle endured the longest siege in English history. Around this time Simon de Montfort convened Parliament and it may have been held on land now called Parliament Piece.

This land was given to the Open Spaces Society in 1987 by the landowner, Miss Martin. Nearby, Kenilworth Common is a good place for walking, as are Crackley Woods and the disused railway line. The land is very fertile and coal has recently been found in great abundance below its beauty. Deciding upon the best and most inconspicuous way of mining this black gold is one of fierce debate at the moment.

At the beginning of this century tanning and comb making were local industries but today many people are employed in Coventry, Leamington Spa or Birmingham.

Kineton

Kineton has been established for many centuries. Royal residence gave the village the name of Kington, which is mentioned in the Domesday Book. In feudal times everyone depended on the gentry for their living. Even at the turn of the century the gentry insisted that boys raised their hats and bowed to them while the girls curtsied. The children would go miles out of their way to get out of doing it.

During the 19th century, up to 1890, a cattle market was held in the village Market Square on Tuesdays. The mop fair still comes to the Market Square every year around the 4th October.

There are three public houses in the village, two dating back to the 17th century. Up to 30 years ago there was a fourth public house called The Rose and Crown, dated 1665, which was in the Market Square but that closed down and became a private dwelling.

During the Second World War Kineton was used as a transit camp, with Polish and Czechoslovakian soldiers stationed here. Later soldiers from the Pioneer Corps and REME were stationed in the village. At one time at least the area which is now called Park Piece was covered with large tents.

In 1958 Kineton High School was opened. Children aged 11 and over attended the school and buses were laid on to bring in children from the neighbouring villages. During this time many new housing estates were built, namely St Peters Road, Castle Road and Green Farm Estate.

Kingsbury

There cannot be many villages in Warwickshire – or in the country for that matter – which can boast a sports hall, youth centre, health centre, swimming pool, 12th century church, the remains of a fortified manor house and a school founded in 1686.

Mercia was the principal Saxon kingdom when Offa became king. Tamworth was its capital and the countryside around became the king's hunting ground. A 'bury' (or fortified house) for the king was established on a bluff overlooking the river Tame. But today mention of Kingsbury conjures up pictures of coal-mines, gravel pits, oil terminals, a rifle range and the Water Park. Certainly for the first half of this century, the village economy revolved around the coalmines of nearby Piccadilly and Hurley, and agriculture. However, since the end of the Second World War no fewer than four housing developments have transformed the community. Less than 140 years ago Kingsbury comprised the vicarage, school, mill, four farms, nine shops or public buildings and 17 private residences. The village was then quite self-sufficient and few owned their own houses or their businesses. The major landowner was the then Prime Minister, Sir Robert Peel.

Nowadays the majority of houses are owner-occupied and people commute to Birmingham, Coventry or Tamworth – or beyond. The pits are closed and only a few new industries have replaced them locally. Kingsbury has, however, managed to retain many essential village characteristics, much of the community still shows dedication to either the parish church or the Methodist church and many organisations stem from them.

Kingsbury's association with the famous goes back into the 'romantic' Middle Ages when two feuding families, the Bracebridges and the Ardens, experienced a true-life Romeo and Juliet love-affair. Alice Bracebridge from Kingsbury Hall married – against the wishes of both families – John Arden of Park Hall. John's brother's grand-daughter was Mary Arden, mother of William Shakespeare.

Older villagers remember the frequent floods when the river would rise and spread over the flood plain between Kingsbury and the nearby hamlet of Bodymoor Heath. This didn't stop children coming to school across muddy fields and over the 'planks' – a raised footway which still is in everyday use. Indeed, it is one of the features of the 650 acre Water Park developed from sand and gravel workings. More than 180,000 visitors a year are recorded and they can enjoy fishing in some 19 pools, sailing, watersports of all descriptions, horse riding and caravanning. One primary function of the Park is to preserve wildlife and a nature reserve provides hides for bird watchers.

Schooling in Kingsbury can be said to have started as early as 1637. In 1650 William Dugdale, the antiquarian, founded a school using the Bracebridge Chapel of the parish church. In 1686, Thomas Coton, a wealthy landowner, provided in his will for a school and a schoolmaster's house in Church Lane. That house, now a private residence, received a Commendation and Civic Award following its restoration. Now, the village has three fine schools, all sharing a central position.

Ladbroke 🌿

The small village of Ladbroke is situated 2 miles south of Southam and 12 miles north of Banbury. Since it was by-passed in 1986 it has become a truly rural village.

The village of Ladbroc is mentioned in the Domesday Book. The village then had a population of 252 which is very similar to the present day population.

When asked 'where do you live?' and given the answer 'Ladbroke', the usual comment made is 'I thought that was a bookmakers'. The connection is that in the early 1900s Ladbroke House was occupied by W. H. Schwind. He was very interested in horse racing and is reputed to have had a very good eye for a horse.

When his reputation began to get well known he found it increasingly difficult to get good odds especially if it was known that he was betting. He found a solution to the problem, which involved placing bets by telegram just before a race.

This practice resulted in one bookmaker being unable to meet his obligations to Schwind. Schwind and his partners met the owners of the bookmakers from Southampton Row in London at Ladbroke and agreed to take the firm over, but as part of taking it over, the name was changed to Ladbrokes.

One of Ladbroke's other claims to fame is its connection with the Ladbroke Continental Car Group. This firm was started in the village by Mr Graham Hudson.

Ladbroke church dates back to the 13th century and was totally renovated in 1876 by the famous architect Sir Gilbert Scott. The very beautiful church has in its possession a unique set of communion plate presented by Alice, Duchess of Dudley in the late 17th century.

One of the other landmarks in Ladbroke is Ladbroke Hall. This is an imposing building set in its own lavish grounds. It was once the home of Lord Rootes, the famous car manufacturer and it later became a girls boarding school. Legend has it that there is in existence a ghost known as the 'Lady in Black' who wanders around in the dead of night. In the early 1970s the Hall was one of the first country houses to be converted into self-contained properties.

Lapworth 🌿

The village of Lapworth grew out of the Forest of Arden and this determined its widely scattered dwellings, successors to the isolated farmsteads in forest clearings. Quite unlike the nucleated villages in the south of the county, its centre is elusive. It lies in the triangle formed by the two major roads from Birmingham to Stratford-upon-Avon and Warwick. This has preserved its rural peace – a peace threatened by a motorway through its most ancient lanes.

There are many examples illustrating the history of rural architecture in the much restored farmhouses, now mostly private dwellings: old barns in Lapworth Street, a late 15th century house in Bushwood Common Farm, a 16th century one at Mountford Farm in Church Lane and many more.

The church of St Mary the Virgin is a very fine ancient building.

It is short in length but quite wide having a separate tower and spire. For at least 800 years there has been a church on this site. It is thought to have consisted of a small rectangular stone building in about 1190, this being determined from the 12th century work which remains in the nave. It originally had no aisles, a north aisle was added early in the 13th century and about 50 years later a south aisle was added. Also during the 13th century the chancel was rebuilt and an adjoining north chapel constructed. The type of clock in Lapworth church is found only in the Midlands. Originally installed in the 16th century it had a 'kick start' type striking mechanism and no dial. It has a vertical frame made of wood, not iron, which is most unusual.

The advowson of St Mary's has been in the hands of the scholars of Merton College, Oxford for over 700 years and over the centuries many of the college graduates have occupied the office of rector of the parish.

The schoolhouse which is adjacent to the church was built in 1828 and is basically unaltered, but as early as 1783 a village school was operating on a regular basis in a cottage schoolroom at the edge of the churchyard (this cottage no longer exists).

Lapworth also has explosive connections. The originator of the Gunpowder Plot, Robert Catesby is reputed to have been born at Bushwood Hall in 1573, his father then being the Lord of Lapworth and Bushwood Manors. Catesby appears to have been a gentleman of great force and character. His servant and fellow conspirator, Thomas Bates, was also born in Lapworth and his name can be found in the Lapworth parish register.

The Stratford canal with its large flight of locks and junction pool at Kingswood where it touches the Grand Union Canal has many pleasurable features. Pleasant walks can be made along its banks, numerous ducks and geese find a home there and are always grateful for a piece of bread. During the summer and early autumn the canal is alive with craft of all kinds bearing holiday makers. Many tie up overnight as close by are several shops and two attractive country inns, The Boot and The Navigation, both being very old buildings. Fishermen from a wide area are attracted to the canal towpaths and can be seen in all weathers waiting for a fish to take the bait. Unique to the Stratford-upon-Avon canal are the barrel roofed houses and split bridges. The barrel roofed houses were designed by Josiah Clowes, having it in mind to use the techniques of the canal builders. The split bridges were built of iron in two sections, so that the tow line could pass through the slot between them, therefore saving time and energy.

Leek Wootton 🌿

Even before its mention in the Domesday Book, 1086, the 'wooded hamlet' as its Anglo-Saxon name implies, existed. The charm of Leek Wootton lies in its compact development over recent years – careful in-filling but no ugly sprawl into the surrounding woods and farmlands.

The settlement of 33 families has now grown to over 1,000 residents, and it lies between the castled towns of Warwick and Kenilworth. The main road linking these two good shopping centres (and with a 'bus service too!) carves a line through the village. On the eastern side of the road are the village school, residential estate, Ted Edgar's Ranch House and stables, the Hill Wootton hamlet and farmlands dipping down to the river Avon. Spread along the western side of Warwick Road are the church, post office/shop, The Anchor public house, several large old houses and farms, a small housing estate, and Woodcote Hall, now the Warwickshire Police Headquarters.

A nearby historic monument, hidden in woods high on Blacklow Hill, is a memorial to Piers Gaveston, favourite of Edward II, whose stone cross bears the chilling words – 'Beneath the hollow of this rock, on July 3rd 1312, was beheaded by Barons lawless as himself Piers Gaveston, Earl of Cornwall. A hated minion of a hated king, an instance of misrule.' Well worth a gentle climb, and rewarded in February with a carpet of snowdrops. Another favourite walk is from Guyscliffe, once a mill – where the Avon can be crossed, and up to the unspoilt hamlet and church of Old Milverton.

Between Woodcote and the school lies the Memorial Recreation Ground, with its splendid rural view across to St John's spire at Kenilworth. Amongst other activities, cricket is devotedly played here, and the well-mown grass is kept in perfect condition by Sports Club volunteers. Their club house is soon to be rebuilt. At one corner is the Working Men's Club and the third timber building is the village hall.

On a rising bank above the road stands the church of All Saints, stone built, and replacing an earlier one which was pulled down in 1789; but a church has stood near there since 1122. In the churchyard were buried two stragglers from the Battle of Edgehill. On the grass lies an old Norman font. Lime trees cast their shade and scent over the paths, and for these we can thank the 77 parishioners of 1844 who each planted one! The old bells in the tower are rung, and the fifth and oldest was the work of one Johannes de Stafford in the 14th century. This bell is now wired to the church clock, so the chimes that ring across the meadows could have been heard 600 years ago!

Leek Wootton is the fortunate beneficiary of a charity dating back to 1668, and this is administered as a small but welcome 'bonus' to the 'poor of the Parish' at Christmas. The same benefactor, the Duchess Dudley, Lady Alice, also presented the beautiful communion plate of silver gilt, to the church of All Saints, and in thanksgiving her name is always remembered in church every Whit Sunday.

Lillington

One of the lesser-known distinctions which England can claim is that it has undergone a successful heart transplant – and it took place at Lillington on the outskirts of Leamington Spa. The exact heart of England – if one discounts other neighbouring claimants to the honour – is at the junction of Lillington Avenue and Lillington Road, a hallowed spot marked for centuries by a venerable tree known appropriately as the Midland Oak.

In 1966 with this noble landmark suffering from old age, and the adjacent traffic artery needing widening, England's 'heart transplant' took place. The ancient oak was removed and one of its progeny planted in its place nearby to perpetuate the role of marking the centre of England. Thus is Lillington's principal claim to fame.

The first element of the village's name is derived from 'Lilla', an Anglo-Saxon thegn of Eadwine. The second element, 'tun', signifies a farmstead, so Lillington was Lilla's farm.

Indeed, with only 16 adult inhabitants in 1086, it has been mainly a farming community right up to the present century, when it was united with Leamington Spa. Even today the occasional farm building can still be recognised, part of one group near the church having been converted into garage premises.

From the evidence of the parish records, it would seem that the village escaped the worst ravages of the plague. The 1801 census showed a population of 178, which had increased to over 2,000 by 1931. Today, the figure has grown almost unbelievably to almost 20,000, with many acres of the parish now covered with council and private housing developments.

The first evidence of a parish church is from the records of Kenilworth Priory, when William de Kilkenny was made vicar of Lillington in 1252. The oldest part of the building, which is dedicated to St Mary Magdalene, is the south wall of the chancel, which is of Norman origin. However, the most interesting part of the structure is the tower which was built in the 15th century. Among its eight bells is one dated as early as 1480, while two others date from 1625 and 1675. It is an intriguing thought that a bell which Lillington folk hear rung each week, was ringing out over the same parish before Christopher Columbus discovered America.

The most noteworthy epitaph in the churchyard, and just still legible, is that to the memory of one William Treen, who died on 3rd February 1810, aged 77:

'I poorly liv'd and poorly dy'd
Poorly buried and no one cry'd.'

He was known as 'Old Billy Treen, the miserd'. He is said to have been a road-scraper who existed miserably by begging potato peelings and turnips from the farmers. When he died, however, it was discovered that he had amassed a secret fortune.

There are now very few old buildings left, and the picturesque thatched and timber-framed cottages which graced Cubbington

Road until the late 1960s, one of which was once old Billy Treen's home, are now no more than a nostalgic memory in the minds of older inhabitants. The handsome stone-built Manor House, near the church, has lost most of its land to housing developments, while the former 19th century home of the Unett family, Castel Froma, is now used as a home for the disabled.

It is all a far cry from Lilla's farmstead, and Lillington can certainly not count itself among Warwickshire's most eye-catching villages. But at least it can proudly say it marks the vibrant heart of all England.

Little Wolford 🍃

Little Wolford is an unspoilt hamlet spread along a narrow ridge in the Warwickshire fringes of the Cotswolds. The little cluster of houses and the narrow green make a village so small that many drive through without realising that they have been here. From the village the views are tremendous, over to Brailes Hill in the east and 10 miles to Broadway Tower in the west.

Of the 35 houses, mainly built in Cotswold stone, the oldest and most notable is the Manor, dating from the 15th century, an L-shaped stone house still with its great hall. For about a hundred years this fell into disrepair, and became three cottages while the hall was used as a school, chapel and meeting place. Since its restoration before the Second World War the Manor has been a most attractive private house, and its hall is still a focal point in the village as the present owners hold many fundraising activities for local charities. The restoration has not spoiled the stains on the solar stairs, reputed to be bloodstains from after the battle of Edgehill in 1642.

Nine farmhouses lie in the parish, all originally part of the Weston Estate, as was the village. Only three are now true farmhouses. One of the others had an interesting existence in the Second World War when the actors from the Old Vic company were evacuated there and provided much amusement for the village. One farmhouse has been separated from its barns and the inevitable conversion into houses has taken place – just as some cottages have been amalgamated to make larger houses. People say that a witch used to live in one cottage in the village – perhaps true, as a devil stone was found over the back door there during modernisation.

Just on the edge of the village a tiny lodge designed by the architect of Buckingham Palace and the long-gone Weston House, has stone angels on each corner and a stone devil over the back door. Stone carvings also decorate the two remaining fountains which used to be the main water supply in the village. The larger fountain has a very jumbled coat of arms, and a fine lion's head for the water spout.

Round the village in the many grass fields lie reminders of the past – a long past, since Wolford was mentioned in the Domesday Book. Ridge and furrow from medieval farming still remains, as does the rough ground where the brickyard was, and the line of the old mill stream. Harder to find is the old Glyde Well whose water was said to hold healing properties for sick eyes and ears.

Long Compton 🖾

South of Stratford-upon-Avon and deep into some of the loveliest countryside which England can boast, lies the village of Long Compton. Through the village runs the A34, a road much used by tourists.

As its name implies, it is a very long village, and about half way along its street, surrounded by picturesque cottages in colourful gardens, stands the large church of St Peter and St Paul. Most of the building dates from the 13th century, but there was a much earlier church, possibly with a thatched roof. But what the passing motorist usually notices is the handsome lychgate. In fact this lychgate was a cottage dating from about 1600, with the lower storey removed, partly half timbered with brick infilling. The building was purchased in the 1950s by Mr Latham, a local builder, who restored and reroofed it. In 1964, after Mr Latham's death, his widow handed over the lychgate to the church as a memorial to her husband, and it is now the main entrance to the churchyard.

From a studio in Long Compton, Donald Brooke, an artist in stained glass, sent out his work far and wide.

An earlier example of village craftsmanship was the King's Stone Printing Press, set up in 1922 by the Rev William Manton. A number of books were printed, and during the General Strike of 1926 the Press published the *Long Compton Wireless News*, distributed by drivers throughout Britain.

This printing press derived its name from the King's Stone, one of the Rollright Stones which can be reached by following the A34 up a long hill out of Long Compton. On one side of the road stands the solitary King's Stone, and on the other side are two groups of stones, the Whispering Knights and the Circle. This is the best preserved stone circle in the Midlands, visited by many people every year who come to gaze, to count the stones (very confusing!) and to relate old legends and evil deeds. The truth no one knows. Much has been written about the Stones but the mystery is not solved.

Tradition tells how a king set out to conquer England, and as he came up the hill from Great Rollright he was halted by a witch who told him to take seven long strides and then –

> 'If Long Compton thou canst see
> King of England thou shalt be'.

The king eagerly strode out, but as he took the seventh stride he saw not Long Compton but a long mound of earth which still remains. Said the witch –

> 'As Long Compton thou canst not see
> King of England thou shalt not be.
> Rise up stick, and stand still, stone,
> For King of England thou shalt be none.
> Thou and they men hoarstones shalt be,
> And I shall be an eldern tree'.

So the king became a standing stone, and his followers on the other side of the road likewise became monoliths.

Long Lawford 🦢

When William the Conqueror compiled the Domesday Book in 1086 the village was called Leileford and held by Geoffrey de Wirce, who in 1077 founded a small priory of Benedictine monks at what was later Monks Kirby. The abbey was bequeathed to the monks of Pipewell in 1160, who were Lords of the Manor for over 400 years.

By 1332 Leileford had become Longa Lalleford and was the largest settlement in the whole district. When Henry VIII abolished the monastery in 1542 the Grange of Long Lawford and other lands were granted to Edward Boughton. Lawford Hall, the home of the Boughtons, dominated the life of the village for the next two centuries, until the murder there in 1780 of Sir Theodosius, the last male heir of the Boughtons. The hall was sold to the Caldecott family, who pulled it down as 'a thing accursed' and built Holbrook Grange on the opposite side of the river and much closer to the village.

The church of St John was built in 1839 by John Caldecott as a Chapel of Ease to Newbold church and was intended mainly for the use of the servants from Holbrook Grange. The furnishings are quite rare as the pews, pulpit and the reading desk are the original ones installed by John Caldecott and have hardly changed.

The Church Hall next door was built in 1939 on land given by Herbert Kay, headmaster of the village school for many years. The bricks of the hall bear the initials of the Sunday School children and others who each bought a brick to help build the hall.

The village has changed since those times, although many old buildings remain. Among these is the Saracens Head, now much modernised, but where in the 1800s some of the council meetings were conducted. Another building in Main Street, now a house, was the village bakery. It was in the hands of the Garratt family for hundreds of years and was where the villagers brought their Sunday dinners to be cooked by the baker for one penny. The Yorkshire pudding was taken along in a jug, to be put in at 12 o'clock. Most people kept a pig and when it was killed, brought pies and faggots in a wheelbarrow to the baker for cooking in his large ovens. Among the pies was one 'Boney Pie', made of the backbone of the pig.

It was here in the bakery that Captain Caldecott lodged with the Garratts for 30 years after leaving the Grange, when he disagreed with his sister over dressing for dinner. Born in 1836 in India he was a fierce looking but kindly man, who insisted on being addressed as Captain. His clothes were those worn by a country squire of 60 years earlier, and he wore a hat with safety pins round the brim to keep off the flies.

The old school has long since been closed and a modern one built, more suitable for today's needs and the expanding population, but it is good to see that the old school has not been pulled down but still retains some of its character as houses.

Now more and more houses are being built, but the centre still has a lot of the old buildings and the feel of a village.

Long Marston 🐦

Long Marston is a small village some 6 miles south-west of Stratford-upon-Avon, lying in the very corner of Warwickshire. The parish boundaries adjoin the counties of Gloucestershire and Worcestershire and in fact the village was originally in Gloucestershire and was transferred to Warwickshire when the boundary was revised in 1931.

It is difficult to know when the first people settled in Long Marston, though it is known that there were early settlements, pre-Roman and Roman, not far away. The name is quite common and 'Marston' is found in several counties. *The Place-Names of Gloucestershire* gives the derivation from the Anglo-Saxon 'macre-stän' – the boundary stone. There is little doubt that a community was established here by the time of the Kingdom of Mercia, and written evidence comes in 1043, when Earl Leofric granted Long Marston to the Monks of Coventry. The main industry of those days was agriculture with the inhabitants working for the monks, who were the Lords of the Manor. The people owned no property nor were they entitled to any wage, but were fed, clothed and housed by the monks.

Between 1200 and 1250 the village was sold to the Cotswold Abbey of Winchcombe. Around 1395 the church was built, although it has been restored and altered since then. In 1539 came the Dissolution of the Monasteries – the Abbey of Winchcombe ceased to exist and the Crown took possession. In 1566 Queen Elizabeth I granted the Lordship and the Manor of Long Marston to Robert, Earl of Leicester, but he did not remain in possession long. In 1577 John Kecke and John Tomes, two yeomen, bought the land and buildings of the Manor.

It may be in these years, at the close of the 16th century, that Shakespeare probably wrote the lines about 'Dancing Marston' (see Temple Grafton).

There is now a local Morris Dancing team, made up of ladies in the village, who go around local villages giving displays.

In 1643 a local man, John Cooper, died and left an amount of money for the erection of a school, which was later called the Grammar School and which survived until 1910.

On a September day in 1651, Charles II was brought to Long Marston in his flight after the battle of Worcester. It was to the Manor House, now known as Kings Lodge, that the King came, dressed as a manservant, and was promptly ordered to wind up the jack on which the meat was to be roasted. The jack is still at Kings Lodge today.

The aerodrome was constructed in 1940. It was never more than a support airfield, with only a few permanent buildings, but its concrete runways are extensive. After the war it was little used, but now is used for drag-racing, motor-bike racing, gliding and microlight flying and has one of the largest Sunday markets in the county. The army camp was a much bigger affair. To give it its full title – No. 1 Engineers' Supply Depot, RE – now called Engineer Resources, it is the largest establishment of its kind in England, storing and maintaining such things as Bailey bridges, pontoons and engineering equipment for the army in England and Germany. During the Falklands War there was great activity over the camp, and the village, with helicopters moving equipment. The camp has now diminished in size, but it was said to have contained 35 miles of railway track within its perimeter at one time. It has provided work, in a great variety of jobs, and in this has proved a great boon to the village.

Today the village is occupied by people who commute, to either Birmingham or Coventry, for their work, but there is still farming and market gardening carried on in the community. There is a large poultry unit in the village and also an equestrian centre that holds events two or three times a year, at which the Princess Royal and other well known riders have taken part.

Loxley

Loxley is a small community. There are some outlying houses and farms, but the huddle of houses on the hillside forms the main part of the village.

During the last 20 years, as is inevitable, there have been changes, although very few physical changes have taken place and few houses have been built. Since 1976, when Loxley was declared a non-development area in the Warwickshire Structure Plan, only barn conversions and extensions to existing dwellings have been allowed.

When newly-weds come out of the church, they find the church gate festooned and tied with trails of ivy. It is the groom's job to open the gate. If he performs this task (his first as a newly married man), without using a knife, legend has it that the couple will have a long and happy married life! The church is named for St Nicholas. It stands on foundations which are amongst the oldest in the country. The site was given to the Cathedral Church of Worcester by Offa, King of Mercia in AD 760. There are several ancient ecclesiastical relics housed in the church. During the spring, the churchyard (in which, reputedly, casualties from the Battle of Edgehill are buried), is carpeted with snowdrops, aconites, blue anemones, violets and primroses and it attracts sight-seers from miles around. On a balmy summer evening at evensong, with the bleating of sheep and lambs from the nearby meadows one really feels at peace with the world.

The village has no buildings of great architectural merit and has no great claim to fame. The Underhill Trust, set up in the year 1780 with the sum of £100 by Mrs Margaret Underhill, for the

96

'benefit and succour of the needy of the Parish' from time to time provides Christmas treats for the elderly. It is the people who make Loxley special and who will continue to do so.

Luddington

Luddington is a very pleasant hamlet just 3 miles from Stratford-upon-Avon, on the river Avon, with beautiful views of the Cots-wolds. Some of the cottages are quite old black and white ones, but a lot of houses have been built since the 1930s.

It is said that William Shakespeare married Ann Hathaway in the old chapel, which was burnt down towards the end of the 18th century. A new church was consecrated in 1872, built on land given by the Marquis of Hertford, a major landowner. All records in the old church were destroyed with the exception of the Bishops Bible dating from 1591 and the old stone font, which have been carefully preserved.

About 16 years ago the Avon Trust deepened the river to make it navigable for pleasure boats, a lock was built and there are now moorings. Unfortunately this has made a vast difference to the wildlife on the river, but on the other hand there is now less risk of flooding. The floods come up quickly but they are down again in a couple of days. There is a right of way along the river bank and it is possible to walk to Stratford.

Luddington is a very friendly place and is fortunate to have a village hall, built in 1957 on land given by Mr C. H. Whitehead. There is no shop or pub. Luddington did not have electricity until 1950 and now with overhead cables has to be prepared for cuts in the supply, as snow, heavy frost, winds or thunderstorms can bring the cables down. The village has been cut off in the depth of winter for more than 60 hours.

In the evenings, just as the sun is going down, a beautiful light comes over the land. It lasts only 5 minutes and is a delight to stand and watch.

Mancetter 🌿

Mancetter is situated on a rocky outcrop overlooking the valley of the river Anker. The name Mancetter comes from the Roman Mandueffedum. This was a Roman camp on the slight rise on which the church now stands. It was one of a line of forts built as the Romans advanced northwards, the A5 (Watling Street) marking the frontier.

William the Conqueror granted the Manor of Mancetter to his nephew the Earl of Chester, who bestowed it on a Norman knight. He assumed the name of Mancestre and built the church and manor house.

Mancetter Manor was a 14th century house of massive oak framing. Extensions and additions to the front now make it look like a half-timbered gabled house of the Tudor period. Here lived the Mancetter Martyr, Robert Glover and his brothers John and William. They were active Protestants at a time when Mary Tudor was trying to impose Catholicism on England. Robert, ill in bed at the time, was arrested and was burnt at the stake in Coventry in 1555. John and William escaped, but died of starvation.

A neighbour, Mrs Lewis, also a Protestant, was hidden in a little room off the main bedroom in Manor Farm, but she was eventually burnt at the stake in Lichfield in 1557. There are secret panels in the Manor and a secret passage from Mancetter to Merevale.

Between the Manor and the church are a row of almshouses, which along with another row opposite the church, were built in 1728 and endowed from the money, £2,000, left by James Gramer, a London goldsmith of Atherstone descent. The cottages were only for men of at least three score years, honest and good churchmen who lived in Mancetter or Atherstone. There are several parochial charities. One is Martin's Charity, recorded on a tombstone in the churchyard, which refers to the gift of a gray coat and hat for poor people each year.

Guy de Mancestre started building the first part of the church tower in the 14th century but he died in 1365 before it was finally completed in the 15th century. The north aisle of the church was the chapel of the Bracebridges of Atherstone. The south aisle was the chantry of the convent of Merevale. The east window contains fine stained glass and is thought to have been part of the great Jesse window from Merevale Abbey. Part of this window was made by John Thornton, builder of the great east window of York Minster.

As trade developed in Norman times so the town of Atherstone gradually grew in size and the importance of the village of Mancetter slowly diminished, although the church of Mancetter still remained the mother church.

The Dame School was in a cottage where scholars were charged two pence per week. The present school was built in 1875 with one room only and additions were made as the number of children increased.

There are only two pubs in the village. The 14th century Plough Inn was next to the church and one of the cottages adjacent to it was thought to be the Guild House set up by the Abbot of Merevale. The Blue Boar Inn was a small place near the smithy and the old Arbor cottages.

The lovely countryside around Mancetter was part of the Arden Forest and by 1779 there were five mixed farms in the area. Hospital Farm was once the Fever Hospital. Stoneleigh Glebe Quarry Farm is very old with a date of 1714 scratched on a brick. On one chimney is a bell which could be rung by the farmer if he was being attacked by thieves! Many of the fields round the village are now housing estates, but there is a large recreation ground where a stream runs through. On the outskirts of the village are delightful areas of countryside to walk through: the Outwoods, Blue Bell Woods, Purley Chase, and round the reservoir.

The retaining dam of the reservoir was lined with stone from the Mancetter quarry which was started in the 19th century. Two quarries merged in 1951 and now it is a modernised industry producing over 1,000 tons a day. Many of the local men work at the quarry and also at the coal pits just north of Atherstone. A small industrial estate was set up between Mancetter and Atherstone with light industries, which also employ local people.

Marton 🍂

Marton stands at the confluence of the rivers Leam and Itchin and is dissected by the A423, Coventry to Oxford road. An interesting feature here is the 'Middleton Bridge' over the river Leam, named after John Middleton who was born in the village but became a wealthy mercer in the City of London at the time of Sir Richard (Dick) Whittington. it was built in 1414, possibly to celebrate his retirement as Warden of the Ancient Mercers' Company, and by his intervention the villagers were released from the payment of toll. It is unusual in that it follows the curve of the road and although widened and improved to accommodate modern traffic some of the original stone arches can still be seen. Within the village a private road to Hockley House Farm crosses the river Itchin via a bridge built by Samual Shepherd around 1850.

The parish church is dedicated to the Holy Spirit, itself uncommon, but unique here in that the French form, St Espirt, is used. This arises from the granting of the church in the 12th century by King Stephen as a Chapel of Ease to a French order of nuns originating in Fontvrallt, later installed in Nuneaton. When nearby land was being excavated for building some years ago, several ancient bones were exhumed which experts at Warwick County Museum thought were those of some of the nuns, the dating and location coinciding with the time during which the Chapel of Ease existed here. This may have a connection with curious rumours of ghostly nuns being seen in Marton, at least one sighting being quite authentic, even though inexplicable. The church was destroyed, possibly by fire, in the 1860s and rebuilt in 1871, although some of the original ancient structure remains.

The village boasts its own Museum of County Bygones, run by a local historian, George Tims, where many artifacts from days gone by, agricultural and domestic, can be seen, all beautifully displayed in a specially constructed building.

There is also a strong artistic flavour to the community. Marton Artists, a group of talented local people, hold annual exhibitions to display the work of painters, a ceramic artist, a potter, a wood turner, a cartoonist and knitwear designer, some of whom are establishing an international reputation.

100

Two local butterfly and moth enthusiasts were able during the 1970s to advise the Warwickshire Biological Records Centre of the first recorded Warwickshire sighting of the Varied Coronet (*Hadena Compta*), a Dewicks Plusia (*Mcdunnoughia Confusa*) and a Silver Striped Hawk Moth (*Hippotion Celerio*), the latter the only Warwickshire sighting this century. There is also a colony of Marbled White butterflies, not scarce but rarely seen because they live in very local colonies. Also in the area of natural history, there is still an ancient ridge and furrow field to be seen in the village.

Many interesting and talented people have contributed to the life of the village over the years, and notable among them were Noel and Barbara Newsome, both talented artists who had exhibited at the Royal Academy. Noel had had a fascinating career, including service with the Ministry of Information during the war and during his time here he worked tirelessly for the village, its church and for conservation. Barbara became the first woman churchwarden at Marton church and her talent as a sculptor was displayed whenever sufficient frozen snow enabled her to do exquisite snow sculptures round the village, which brought traffic chaos when people from miles around came to view them. She also produced large numbers of sunfaces, moulded in cement, and almost every garden in the village boasts one of these.

Another famous inhabitant of Marton in the past was a race-horse foal named Santa Claus, bred by the local doctor, Frank Smorfitt, which went on to win the Derby in 1964. After feeding him with apples and crusts of bread and watching him career round the paddock after his dam, the villagers cheered him to a man on that June day.

Maxstoke 🐗

In the Domesday Book the village was called 'Machitone'. In 1170 according to Pipe Rolls it was 'Makestoke'. This part of Warwickshire was forest and would account for the meaning of a place ending with 'stoke', meaning stockade. Stockades were built as fences for animals for safety from intruders and wolves. 'Max' was from a local word known as 'Macca'.

Sir William de Clinton who built the castle – now lived in by Captain and Mrs Fetherston Dilke – founded a 'chantry' on the site of the church in 1333, and dedicated it to St Michael and All Angels. A chantry was an endowed chapel where masses for the dead were sung. In 1342 he developed it into a priory, which played a vital part in the local economy. It kept beef and dairy herds and its produce was sold at Coleshill Market.

In the 1980s the village is much as it was, except that the school has now closed. The golf club is now where the prisoner of war camp was built in the Second World War, overflowing into the park, a much loved place for walks. The village still has its characters – Charlie the mole catcher, with his dry sense of humour, can do any job you want him to and will always have a tale to tell. He will always be particularly remembered for his work of relaying the path of the church – a real work of art.

The farms are now edged with a motorway and criss-crossed with gas and fuel pipelines, and underneath all that is a coal mine, but still the farmers carry on.

Middleton 🐿

This village is like an island, situated in a network of motorways. Hamlets, e.g. Hunts Green, Allen End, Hill Lane, cover a radius of 15 miles and make up the village. Middleton is five miles from Tamworth and five miles from Sutton Coldfield, and the name probably indicated the midway position between these two towns.

Both the church and the village are recorded in the Conqueror's Domesday Book. The village school which was built in 1886 was originally a Church School, and had as many as 100 pupils at one time. Twice the school has been reprieved from closure.

The church is St John The Baptist and goes back to Anglo Saxon times. No trace of the Saxon church remains, for the church was rebuilt in the Norman style, probably towards the end of the 12th century. The church which has a tower, once had a steeple. The nave is divided from the chancel by a fine medieval screen. On the north wall of the chancel is the 'Lepers Squint'. There is a sculpture of two half brothers, Benjamin and Samuel White, whose father, Samuel White, was one of the principal benefactors of Middleton. The story is that one day he passed through the village and saw some hungry looking children. He was so moved by this that he decided to give money for the poor of the parish. As a result of his benefactions, six almshouses have been built (1966) and doles were distributed to the widows, the old and the needy, and at Whitsuntide every child received a Whit loaf. Now only the village school children receive a loaf during a special school Whitsuntide service in the church. The original base of the cross still remains in the churchyard.

The Lady Middleton Charity and Middleton United Foundation are two charities for the young and the old of the village. Lady Middleton left money for a bible to be given to every school leaver. Middleton United Foundation gives help for educational expenses of the young students of the village.

For many generations the Willoughby family occupied Middleton Hall. The Hall had two Royal visitors. Queen Elizabeth I, who it is said called on her way to Coventry and gave Sir Hugh Willoughby his Knighthood, and James I, who stayed there on his journey from Scotland and knighted Sir Percival Willoughby who had then inherited the Hall. Hugh Willoughby was an explorer. The Hall was a moated residence, but in the year 1868 the occupier decided to do away with the moat. It is now being restored back to a moated residence. A skeleton of a horse and rider in armour was discovered in the moat and the rider was thought to be a Courier 'Messenger' in the Royalist Army when the battle of Edgehill in Warwickshire was fought on 23rd October 1642 and that the rider was leaving the hall one night in a dense fog when he lost his bearings and instead of making for the bridge, crossed the quadrangle and tripped over the parapet into the moat. The human bones were buried in the churchyard and the gauntlet glove and helmet are displayed in the chancel of Middleton church. Mr John Ray who stayed in Middleton Hall in 1666 as a tutor, was a naturalist. Ray's plant records from the Middleton neighbourhood contribute almost 40 of the first species recorded for Warwickshire plus some first species recordings for the British Isles dating from his works at Middleton.

In 1966, the last tenants of the Hall were the Averill family and they moved out due to the state of gradual deterioration. In 1978, Mr Peter Thomas of The Vicarage, Middleton, formed a trust known as Middleton Hall Trust. This Trust has gone from strength to strength and now has a large membership. The building is being repaired and improved. Many evening and week-end events take place. Bird hides have been erected and the wall garden restored.

The Village Stocks were located next to the Green Man public house. This building was once a farmhouse and a family named Stevenson were publicans for 100 years. There was a club room in the public house, which was used for the rents to be paid.

Most villages have their ghosts and Middleton is no exception. Residents talk of a figure dressed in black silk walking from the church to a nearby cottage every Hallowe'en!

Moreton Morrell 🌿

Nestling equi-distant from Warwick, Leamington Spa and Stratford-upon-Avon, Moreton Morrell is a charming village of new and old – old being very old, thatched roofs and wattle and daub walls. Even the road names are interesting. For example Duffus Hill, the main road through the village. Did dovehouses really exist here? Fullers Place is named after the people who once kept the post office.

On the outskirts of the village is the Agricultural College. This seems to grow every year and is probably the largest employer in the village. The Agricultural College was originally a large house, and having built the house, the owner decided to build a Real Tennis court which is housed in a large building directly opposite the college entrance.

There is a village pub, The Black Horse, which some years ago was called The Sea Horse. What a misnomer for a public house so close to the middle of England! A good hostelry nonetheless, friendly and a splendid cold table.

The village school is a Church of England School with about 70 pupils taken from Moreton Morrell and the surrounding villages. Because of an increase in pupils the temporary classroom is likely to become permanent. The old school is now the village hall.

On the extreme edge of the village, the church of the Holy Cross is a beautiful building dating back to the Domesday Book. Services are held here on a regular weekly rota alternating between Communion, Matins, Family Service and Evensong. It's the Family Service you must come to, to see just how much fun young children get from attending church – but only through the patience of the curate and the understanding of the congregation.

Napton ⚜

For centuries two buildings have dominated the skyline of Napton village: high above the houses rise the outlines of the ancient church and the impressive windmill. Seven counties are said to be visible from the top of the 500 foot high hill on a fine day. It is probable that an Iron Age fort once crowned its summit.

The name Napton means 'village on the hilltop', from the Anglo Saxon 'cnaepp' meaning hilltop and 'tun' a settlement. It is recorded as Neptone in the Domesday Book. By the Middle Ages it had become one of the three largest towns in Warwickshire. Unusually, the population then was almost the same as it is today with approximately 1,000 people living within its boundaries. It possessed at least three manors and a charter was granted by Edward II in the 14th century giving it the right to hold a weekly Thursday market and an annual three day fair. Neither market nor fair exist any longer. In many places in and around Napton may be seen extensive medieval strip systems where long departed villagers grew their crops and it remains basically an agricultural community. Unlike much of Warwickshire, Napton was not part of the vast Forest of Arden but it was 'feldon' or agricultural land which was not densely wooded. Local houses were stone built and not timbered as in neighbouring areas.

The De Napton family lived in one of the long lost manors until their last heir, a girl named Jana, married one of the Shuckburgh family during the 14th century. Since that time Napton and

105

Shuckburgh, 2 miles distant, have been linked in many ways and they are now part of the same parish together with neighbouring Stockton.

The church of St Lawrence dates from the 12th century, it was rebuilt in the 13th century and has later additions. In common with several other hilltop villages, there is a legend which tells how the original church was to have been built near to the present village green. Each night, however, the stones which lay ready for its construction were transported by 'fairies' or 'spirits' to the summit of Napton Hill. The villagers took the hint and the church duly arose on the hill-top overlooking the village nestling below. Its squat tower has withstood the buffeting winds for centuries.

The church has six bells and these are regularly rung by a team of enthusiastic bell-ringers who occasionally enjoy the challenge of a quarter peal. An old set of hand bells exist and their sweet notes still ring out joyfully at Christmas and other festivals. Napton possesses its very own Christmas carol entitled, *Fleecy Care*. This was probably written by a local person in the late 18th or early 19th century, and it was sung with great gusto by local men during the festive season, often after their tonsils had been well oiled by ale.

The old Methodist chapel has been converted into a unique Nickelodeon or Organ Museum and theatre which is visited by people from all over the country. The Christadelphian chapel on Pillory Green is still in use and the Congregational chapel is now a private house.

Chapel Green, on the edge of the village is named after a 14th century chapel which once stood on the site. Nothing of it remains but excavations have revealed Roman and Saxon relics and it is probable that an earlier village was situated here. Nearby, is the Old Welsh Road, along which drovers walked their cattle from the distant Welsh hills to the markets of Buckingham and London.

The most dramatic building in Napton is undoubtedly the windmill, which was restored in recent years. Originally there were two mills and old maps clearly show them situated quite close together. Records of the mill date back to 1543 but it is probable that an earlier mill existed on this site. A spring and well lie within its grounds going deep down into the hillside and providing a never failing supply of pure water.

There is a footpath leading from the windmill down to what used to be the Napton Brick and Tile works where a large proportion of villagers used to earn their living. Bricks and tiles, marked with the windmill stamp, were produced from local clay and fired in the longest kiln in Europe. These were transported by canal boats which were moored alongside the works on the Oxford Canal. A small industrial estate now occupies the site.

Napton Locks

The Oxford Canal, constructed in the 18th century, sweeps around Napton on three sides and it is a contour canal and not a 'cut' which follows the lowest natural features of the countryside, creating a pleasant meandering route unlike most other waterways. During the 1950s the canal was in danger of being abandoned but the coming of pleasure craft saved its life and now colourful narrow boats ply its length and three marinas bring pleasure and employment to the area. The Grand Union and Oxford Canals join up at Napton and the old wide basins provided for converting boats remain. Old boatmen, often transporting Napton bricks, used Napton windmill as a landmark.

Newbold-on-Avon

In step with other villages, people and places in Newbold have changed dramatically over the years. Cottages on the main street, which, until just before the Second World War, had to get their water from pipes on the pavements outside, have been replaced by a garage. New shops include an 'up-to-date' butchers owned by a local family started in the 1930s, a refrigerator show-room, and two shops selling videos. The village school, built around the middle 1800s, nowadays serves as the village hall following the transfer of the education side of junior life to modern schools. Newbold Rugger Club has a certain standing in the Midlands, especially with the tradition and proximity of Rugby School where it all started.

St Botolph's church stands just below the summit of a hill, overlooking the village. It was built in the 15th century on the site of an earlier church. To the right of the chancel arch can be seen part of the early 14th century tiled floor of the previous church. An incised slab under the arch in the south wall is to Thomas and Elizabeth Boughton and is dated 1454. It may be that this arch tomb indicates that they were responsible for the rebuilding of the church at that time. The organ is dated about 1800 and is believed to have come from Rugby School chapel in 1858. The tower contains eight bells. The clock, dated 1795, is by Sam Dalton of Rugby, and the weathervane, designed in 1975, represents St

Botolph, the original patron saint of travellers, with his pack-donkey.

Diagonally across the churchyard can be seen the sunken line of an old arm of the Oxford Canal which served brickworks and quarries between Newbold and Rugby. This was closed in 1840, but one end of the tunnel can be seen from the field behind the tower. The Oxford Canal flows past the village through one of the longest tunnels in the area – roughly a quarter of a mile. Years ago the canal was used to carry coal, by horse and barge, all over the Midlands. Now it is used for leisure with motorised barges and boats. This brings a lot of visitors to the village and increased business to the local shops.

At one time the top half of the village was closed off by a gate across the road and now on one corner is one of the three public houses. The other two were quite old establishments, now somewhat restored.

New housing estates have sprung up, increasing the population very considerably on either side of the river Avon. The river used to flood quite a part of the village until a new bridge was erected and alleviated the problem.

Newbold-on-Stour

The village of Newbold-on-Stour probably started as a cluster of cottages around a toll house and inn (both still standing), 6 miles south of Stratford-upon-Avon on the road to Shipston-on-Stour and Oxford. It is still not much more. Most buildings are Georgian or Victorian or later.

An exception is Ettington Park which, despite its name, is at the northern end of Newbold. The Victorian house, recently restored after a fire, is an hotel, but it and the park are owned by the Shirley family, who are believed to be the only family left who can claim to still own the land they held at the Norman Conquest.

Also on Shirley land alongside the river Stour is the headquarters of Newbold-on-Stour Sea Scout Troop, which is the sea scout troop furthest from the sea. Founded in 1957 and still thriving, the troop is one of the select band of 100 holding Royal Navy recognition, with annual inspections over more than 25 years.

The village made local news in 1912 with a devastating fire. A row of cottages with thatched roofs opposite the Victorian parish church caught fire and sparks travelled about 100 yards to another row of thatched cottages and they were all destroyed. A horse-drawn manual fire engine was taken down a track to the river and hoses led to the fire, but without effect. Those cob-walled cottages have been replaced with brick-walled, slate-roofed houses, now mainly occupied by commuters.

The only thatched building left in the village is known as the bothy, probably 300 years old. It has thick cob walls and has recently been rethatched. It stands on the village green near the village hall, which was built to replace a wooden hut in the 1950s. The dividing line between the common and Shirley land passes through the foundations. As the Shirleys did not wish to part with any of their long-held land, rights had to be negotiated.

The river Stour provided power for a large number of mills. All are now gone or converted into residences, but the last to go was Talton Mill, where Mr H. Holberton now farms and sells produce.

A notable village craftsman was the saddler Mr J. Rimell, with a reputation that brought in work from a wide area. He had a regular standby contract to make large numbers of martingales to take horse brasses made in Birmingham and sold in America. He died in 1975, but a village road is named after him and his apprentice continues the trade under his name in Shipston-on-Stour.

At Armscote on the south side of the village there is a Quaker Meeting House, which attracts Quakers from all over the country on the first Sunday in August each year, as it was one of the last stopping places of William Fox, when he was being hounded across the country.

About 1910 Primitive Methodists held meetings in the kitchen of the end cottage of the row later burned down. It is said the preacher sat on the copper and the congregation sat on forms. They built the Methodist church, which is hard against the busy A34 road. Because of the noise there, the present congregation holds most services in a chapel at nearby Blackwell. This must be the only church membership of 10 which uses two buildings!

Membership of the church school in the village dwindled and

closure was threatened several times, but the number of children in the village has increased and the school is linked with that at Tredington under one headteacher.

The Victorian parish church is at the stage where considerable maintenance has to be done. The rector also has Tredington Parish and lives there. What was the Newbold rectory, is known as The Grange and is the largest house in the centre of the village. It was built in the days of Victorian opulence, when the rector must have had large numbers of servants. It is now a private residence.

Newbold Pacey & Ashorne

Newbold Pacey is the older of the two places, Newbold Pacey being at one time the village and Ashorne the hamlet. Local folklore says that Ashorne came about when a gentleman named Edward Carew came to Newbold Pacey to escape the plague in London, but brought it with him. The villagers then crossed Oozley Brook to escape the plague and built their houses in Ashorne. Ashorne is an Anglo-Saxon word for north-east, so it signifies the north-east corner of the parish.

There is a monument to Edward Carew and his infant daughter in the church. This monument was brought from the previous church which was partly wooden. The present church was designed by J. L. Pearson, who was also the architect of Truro cathedral. There are a few interesting monuments in the church, one to a past vicar who was nephew of the poet Southey and another to somebody who was,

'a martyr to the gout.'

It is rumoured that a lot of the cottages in Newbold Pacey were burnt down and never rebuilt so that only a few remain today. The old vicarage has an exact replica in Virginia, USA. In Ashorne the oldest houses are around the Green, except Stonehouse Farm House, which is mentioned in the Domesday Book. Several of the houses are wattle and daub, the marl being collected from the

'Holloway', which is now a 'C' class road. At one time this was the only way in and out of the village.

In recent times the village has built a new Village Hall, which replaced a hut dating from the First World War. Unfortunately, the village has lost its school, post office and shop. The chapel has been sold and converted into a house.

One of the local large houses, Ashorne Hill, was once owned by Mr Bryant of Bryant and May Matches, and was bought by the iron and steel industry during the Second World War as their headquarters. It is now a management college.

There is a cricket field which is the only one in the country where you cross water to get from the pavilion to the field. In the adjoining Ashorne House, at one time, lived Major Bouch, whose uncle was the builder of the doomed Tay Bridge.

As in countless English villages, Newbold and Ashorne now has little to offer in the way of employment. Thus, families which have lived in the parish for many generations must look elsewhere for jobs. As they commute to nearby towns, so do the newcomers to the village. There are still a significant number of family names which also appeared in the 1851 census, and whose grandparents feature, as children, in the 1869–70 Log Book of the village school.

Newton Regis

This is the northernmost parish in Warwickshire, the name of which probably derives from its former royal ownership under Henry II (reigned 1154–1189). It has also been known as Kings Newton, and, more picturesquely, as Newton-in-the-Thistles (from early in the 18th century). It is not known whether these were abundant wild thistles or specially-grown teasles, used in the carding of flax fibre for linen production. Flax was grown in Newton and linen looms worked in the house now The Queens Head inn.

The village boasts another royal connection. King Charles I prayed at the church before going into battle towards the end of his reign (1647).

The cathedral in Birmingham was indirectly named after a Newton Regis family. The Phillips family of Newton Hall owned property in Birmingham, and it was Robert Phillips who gave the site of the church, as well as contributing towards its building, 1711–1725. St Philip's church became the cathedral in 1905. The Phillips family married into the Inge family of Thorpe Constantine, just over the border in Staffordshire. Much of Newton Regis is owned by the Thorpe Estate, which built the village school in the 1840s, and also the Institute, or Church Room.

The church, which contains much of historical interest, was originally a chapel to the church at Seckington. The present building is basically 14th century. A singular feature of the village is 'the rock', an outcrop of stone worn into terraces, alongside the pavement opposite the church. The picturesque duck pond in the middle of the village is a quarry pit into which a stream was diverted. A variety of ducks now benefit from this former water supply to the village. They have had a special sign erected by the Council to warn motorists of the habit of the ducks of processing across the road to the farmyard where they live.

There are two public rooms in Newton Regis: the previously mentioned Church Room, and the Village Hall, once the pavilion erected by the Newton Regis Cricket Club, founded in 1858. There is a public house, a village shop and post office, and a craft shop in a converted dairy. This is a friendly and sociable village with up to a dozen clubs and societies. In 1986 and 1987 the village was voted 'Best kept small village in the County of Warwickshire'.

A former festival which may be revived was the Newton Wake, celebrated in October at St Luke's tide until at least the early part of this century. In Victorian times the festival took the form of stalls and 'skittles for a goose' in the inn yard, followed by a dance in the evening.

This is one of the least spoilt villages in North Warwickshire, whose imposing farmhouses and half-timbered thatched cottages have not been obscured by recent small developments.

No Man's Heath 🖎

No Man's Heath is a small village on the A453 with a short but interesting history. Before the last century No Man's Heath was heathland which belonged to neither of the adjoining parishes. A community of 'squatters' developed and the church was built in 1863. By 1871 the population was 122. Some residents still remember the 'mud hut', a thatched one-storey cottage that stood where the Community Centre now is.

One of the first residents of No Man's Heath was Joe Leavesley, a leper. He worked as a coal heaver, and a former Newton Regis resident, Thomas Riley (born 1847), who remembered him described him thus: 'How I looked with dread at the poor man's arm inflamed and scaly as with sleeve turned up he went about his work as a coal heaver with his horse and cart'. He goes on: 'He was the first I believe to build a hut on No Man's Heath, on the Heath itself, not on the fringe of it, in defiance of a neighbouring squire.'

The public house, The Four Counties, records the fact that No Man's Heath used to be the meeting point for the four counties of Warwickshire, Staffordshire, Leicestershire and Derbyshire. The border of Derbyshire has now moved a few miles away, but this heathland became a convenient escape route for fugitives from the law to cross over into a neighbouring county and so evade capture. It was also the site of many prize fights in the 19th century, perhaps for the same reason.

Norton Lindsey 🖎

The south Warwickshire village of Norton Lindsey is surrounded by open countryside, and lies 4 miles away from the county town of Warwick, and 6 from Stratford-upon-Avon. The adult population, according to the electoral roll, numbers just over 300.

The nucleus of the village is around the main street and the road leading to the church. The majority of the older houses are in this area. Their names bear witness to the former nature of the village:

Barn Cottage, The Old Barn, Stable Cottage, The Old Forge, and so forth. Most of the former farmhouses, such as The White House, have shed their land, and only one working farm, Cannings, remains in the centre of the village, though there are others on the periphery. Further from the centre the proportion of old (mostly refurbished) houses to new decreases. A spate of house building about 1968 relates to the time when the sewerage scheme was completed and septic tanks became things of the past.

Traditionally Norton Lindsey has always had links with other villages. At one time the church was associated with Claverdon. Since 1925, the parish has formed part of the United Benefice of Norton Lindsey, Wolverton, and Langley. The rector lives at Wolverton.

The village school, Wolverton Junior and Infants, was built in 1876 near the boundary of the two parishes to provide for the children of Norton Lindsey and Wolverton. To the great joy of the inhabitants the school has survived a threat of closure.

Holy Trinity church dates back to the 13th century. It stands in an oasis of peace and quiet, surrounded by the churchyard and the garden of rest. Its beauty was specially celebrated in 1984 when there was a flower festival which gave great pleasure to the many visitors, and raised money for the new organ which is now installed in the church.

The western gales account for the village's nickname of 'Windy Lindsey', and they will have done their share in turning the sails of the village windmill, which was built between 1793 and 1800, falling into disuse, it is thought, in 1906. It was here that an unfortunate miller, William Blakeman, died as a result of a fall while setting the sail cloths, on 14th March, 1892. Now the mill forms an interesting feature in the garden of the Mill House. It is visited occasionally by windmill enthusiasts.

Less pleasing in appearance than church or mill is the village hall, of timber construction, which in 1966 replaced an earlier building of 1948 vintage. The hall is the focus for the secular activities of the village, some of which are shared with its neighbours. Adjacent to the hall is the village's magnificent playing field acquired in 1948 under terms that require that the land shall not be built on.

Watkins Rose Nursery came in 1960 and left in 1984. With Watkins went what was virtually the only employment within the village, and also the welcome crop of summer visitors who came to see the rose gardens. In 1973 the village shop and post office closed, but people speak of it, and mourn it, as though it were only yesterday. The village once had two pubs, now it has only one, The New Inn. The historic Red Horse was demolished in 1970, a sacrifice to a road-widening scheme.

Old Milverton

It may well be that 'all roads lead to Rome', but only two roads lead to Old Milverton – Old Milverton Lane (a right turn when travelling from Kenilworth to Leamington Spa), and Old Milverton Road (a left turn when approaching Leamington Spa from Warwick), and where these two roads converge there is Old Milverton village.

St James' church marks the end of the route for cars but there are pleasant walks across the fields to the Saxon mill at Guy's Cliffe or into Leamington Spa via Rock Mill Lane. It is said that there is an underground passage from the church to Manor Farm, where, until 1940, there was a 9-hole golf course. The church cemetery contains the graves of the parents of Shirley Williams, the politician, Sir George Catlin and Vera Brittain, the author of *Testament of Youth* and campaigner for feminist rights. Dr Henry Jephson is also buried there. He was a local doctor and regarded almost as the 'patron saint' of Leamington Spa. He helped to establish the high reputation and fame of the town as a spa and its loveliest gardens are named after him.

The fields – Cottage Close, Church Paddocks, Bull Field by the river Avon, Mossy Meadow, and the Pound where stray animals would be held (it lies near to today's bus shelter) – surround only few houses. There is no inn or shop, and never has been in living memory, although at one time there was a post office in the front room of a cottage.

The village is part of the Heber Percy estate and members of the family had the Parish Room, or village hall, built for use as a

The Parish Church of St James, Old Milverton

Sunday School. Opposite the hall is an ancient barn, which retains an old warning 'Man traps and spring guns on these premises.'

Lady Percy used to present Old Milverton girls with red cloaks and the boys with blue jerseys to keep them warm on the long walk into Leamington Spa to go to shool.

The big day in the village is the Horticultural Show and Fete, usually held on the first Saturday in September, when the normally quiet, narrow lane is filled with the cars of visitors and exhibitors.

Over Whitacre 🌿

Over Whitacre is a quiet country parish in the gently rolling hills of north Warwickshire, halfway from everywhere to anywhere: Birmingham to the west, Tamworth to the north, and Atherstone, Nuneaton and Coventry to the east and south. The population is still about the 300 or so of a hundred years ago, but there are now few farm labourers and most people go to the towns to work. Daw

Mill Coal Mine, one of the most modern in the country, lies within the parish, but fortunately it is tucked down into a valley so that only the lights at night are obvious.

One of the old buildings of the village is the Mill, once water driven for iron smelting by the wealthy north Warwickshire Jennens family. It was Charles Jennens who wrote the libretto for Handel's *Messiah*.

At the top of the hill, with a breezy view for many miles, is the 18th century 'squire's' church, built by a squire who wanted something fashionable. He did at least leave a small gem behind when he tore down the medieval church of St Leonard.

An important man in the parish's history was Dr Thomas Bray, who was Perpetual Curate in Charge at the end of the 17th century. Dr Bray was concerned about education and built the first Over Whitacre school-house, which still exists as part of the church hall. Dr Bray was commissioned by the Bishop of London to be 'Commissary to the Colony of Maryland', to organise the colony into parishes, to provide it with clergy, and to provide them with the necessary theological books. Dr Bray was founder of the missionary societies SPCK and USPG. The small house he lived in still exists in the parish.

Oxhill

Oxhill is a name which suggests oxen on a hill, but in fact it is derived from Ohtan Scylf (roughly meaning Ohta's ledge of land, or hill). In the Domesday Book (where a mill is recorded) it is spelled Octeselve. In 1183 Robert de Stafford granted the monks of Bordesley 12 acres of land 'on the torrent (stream) of Oxhill where my oxherds dwell'. It would appear that the homely connection with oxen was brought about as a result of changes in spelling!

At one end of the main street is the Village Hall, originally a Board School, opened in 1876 and closed after the Second World War, since when Oxhill children have travelled to school in neighbouring Tysoe. There is an attractive inn, The Peacock, and further along is the Methodist church, built in 1814 (cottage meetings having been held since 1769) and extended in 1839. Two years later the Sunday School was started, and in 1880 there were celebrations for the centenary of Robert Raikes having founded the first Sunday School (in Gloucester).

At the head of the street is the old church of St Lawrence. There are the remains of a preaching cross near to the north door. The building still retains its original doorways and chancel arch, dating from the mid 12th century. A priest's doorway is probably 14th century, and a 12th century font has curious carvings of Adam and Eve. Not to be missed, at the west end of the church, are six 15th century oak benches, and a fine screen to the tower (originally forming part of a 15th century chancel screen).

In the churchyard, south-east of the church, there is a most interesting little headstone. The inscription is as follows:

'Here lyeth Myrtella, negro body slave to Mr. Thomas Beauchamp, Gent, of Nevis. Bapt. Oct ye 26th and buried ye Jan. 6th 1705'.

Mr Thomas Beauchamp is believed to have been a sugar planter, which would explain this neat headstone, so unexpected in an English village.

Packington

All the inhabitants love this part of the Forest of Arden, whether it be Great or Little Packington. The community existed before the Norman Conquest, many Roman and Stone Age relics having been found. That it was of some prosperity is indicated by the existence of two mills which served a local population of about 60. Its taxation value was 30 shillings, compared with the 20 shillings of its humbler neighbour Birmingham.

The rural church is its focal point. Unfortunately, Little Packington church seems doomed to redundancy. However, Great Packington church still proudly looms large in people's lives. In 1278 the de Clintons of Maxstoke gave it to Kenilworth Priory and thus it remained until the Dissolution of the Monasteries, which gave Henry VIII the opportunity to sell it for £626 to the sitting tenant John Fisher, 'who served with King Henry VIII, King Edward VI, Queen Mary and Queen Elizabeth in Court as Gentleman – Pensioner to them all', a remarkable achievement in such troubled times. Subsequent generations of Fishers served as Lords of the Manor until 1712 when the 2nd Earl of Aylesford married Mary Fisher.

The present building is a strange-looking structure set in the middle of Packington Park. Its appearance belies the beauty of the interior, in which the eye is drawn to the altar-piece by Rigaud, depicting the Ascension. The church is listed on two counts as historically and architecturally important, for in 1789 the building that the Fishers knew was demolished to make way for a brand-new church by the 4th Earl of Aylesford as a public thanksgiving for the recovery of George III from his mental illness.

The building houses a chamber organ designed by Handel for his patron, Charles Jennens, who bequeathed it to his cousins, the Aylesfords. This forms the centre-piece of the annual concert by the Choral and Organ Scholars of King's College, Cambridge. A curious feature in one of the cupolas is the Great Bell. Originally there was a peal of three, but in 1805 the inhabitants in their zealous excitement to celebrate the victory at Trafalgar brought them crashing to the ground. They were melted down to form one Great Bell with a Latin inscription round its lip recalling the mishap, together with a medallion of George III.

There is no actual village in either parish. Great Packington is indicated by no signpost, while Little Packington infuriates all strangers, who are baffled by the way the river bisects its 1,500 acres across which its 14 houses are scattered. Here at the Ford, formerly called Packington Green, before the 18th century Enclosures, the main road from Meriden having passed through the deer park of Great Packington, crossed on its way to Coleshill and Lichfield.

Now there is only one footpath, and not many realise that the medieval due of one shilling is still handed over by the undertaker to the Earl, to permit the passage of a corpse to the churchyard, thus safeguarding the private ownership of the Park, for the free passage of a dead body formerly created a right of way. Indications of former tenants abound in place names: we find Flint's

120

Wood (he was a Catholic who was fined for refusing to go to the Anglican church), Geary's Heath (there was a parson of that name), Dial's Pool, Mulliner's Rough, Butler's End, Todd's Rough and Keatley's Pool. Even more intriguing is Paddy's Path (along the line of an old footpath beside the 'main road') and Jones's Knob – both on rising ground opposite Rookwood, former home of the novelist George Eliot's brother when he was land agent for the Aylesford's Packington estate.

Seven farms surround the 500 acre park and at the northern end lies a 400 acre landfill site, the largest in Europe, from which sand and gravel were formerly extracted and which is now a conservation award winner. Old sand and gravel workings are transformed into a trout fishery and golf course on the eastern borders, also awarded a conservation prize.

The Packingtons today – in spite of being surrounded by a motorway and major trunk roads – continue to be an unspoiled rural community owned by the 11th Earl of Aylesford. Since the devastating fire at Packington Hall in 1979 the Earl and Countess of Aylesford have made the Old Hall their home and their heir, Lord Guernsey, and his family live at the Hall. Both houses stand in the picturesque deer park, home of 400 rare black-backed fallow deer, roaming freely amongst the old woodland and several lakes.

Pailton 🌿

Pailington it used to be. The records of the village and its families go back to the 13th century when Danes and Saxons lived in close proximity if not in complete amity. It is set in beautiful country, an agricultural area where life is perhaps not so rushed as in a town.

Over the centuries the village lands have been divided into various areas and belonged to various Lords of the Manor. Family names going back many years are still found here. Buswell, Bailey, Harrison, Skipworth and of course, the Earls of Denbigh. These names are all on a map dated 1762 which was based on the Pailton enclosure award. Some land was owned by Trinity College, Cambridge, and it held the leasehold and right to collect tithes for a fixed rent from the tenants.

Its church, dedicated to St Denis, was built in 1884 and had a major overhaul in 1982 because of the presence of dry rot. Pailton Hall, in the centre of the village, was left by Lady Mary Feilding, the twin sister of the Earl of Denbigh, to the Archdeacon of Coventry and the Vicar of Monks Kirby for the benefit of 'respectable' inhabitants of the parish of Monks Kirby. The income, at her death, went towards the salary of the curate of the parish. Eventually five trustees were appointed to administer the income and the property. They were responsible to the Charity Commissioners. The Hall was sold in 1986.

Over the years the village has changed of course. The school was bombed during the Second World War and not rebuilt. Since then the schoolchildren have always travelled by bus to the schools in Monks Kirby. The old village hall became a private house and to replace it the Mission Hall in Lutterworth Road was purchased as the new village hall. A few new houses have been built within the village boundaries, older houses have been modernised and fresh blood has come to the village to make a friendly, caring community.

There are two thriving pubs where various village gatherings are held and a village shop which has been in the same hands since 1969. A thriving coach business started from small beginnings by Harry Lewis with a brougham and a dog cart in 1907. He charged 5s.6d to Rugby station and 3s. to Brinklow station. Today his grandson, Norman, has enlarged the business greatly and it is possible to board a luxurious coach in the village and be transported to various parts of Europe and be returned to one's own doorstep.

At the centre of the village where three roads meet, from Coventry, Rugby, and Lutterworth, there used to be a village pump and war memorial but, alas, the pump has disappeared. The village used to have its own bakehouse and it was a great pleasure in the early morning to collect hot bread and watch the dough being put into the baking oven with its glowing fire underneath, and when cooked, taken out with the long handled shovel. Modernisation and the big firms took over and all that remains now is the name The Bakehouse.

Pailton Radio Station was established by the RAF in 1940. 1946 saw it taken over by the Ministry of Civil Aviation. Sputnik I, the first earth satellite, was heard there in October 1957. Since 1946 the buildings have been extended considerably and the number of staff employed has increased.

Polesworth

Polesworth is a large village at the tip of north Warwickshire, bordering on Staffordshire and Leicestershire, and to reach it one has to cross a bridge of some kind. There are two railways, three canals and a wide bridge over the river Anker.

From the river bridge looking eastwards, one can see the beautiful Abbey church and vicarage. The accepted date of the foundation of the Abbey is AD 827. Polesworth got its name from 'Pol' meaning deep water and 'Worth' being dwelling.

It is a place steeped in history. William Shakespeare and Michael Drayton the poet were purported to be visitors to Pooley Hall and The Vicarage. Pooley Hall is an ancient manor house with chapel, overlooking the river and meadows. Thomas Cockayne who built the hall in 1507 was slain on his way to church by his feuding neighbour, Thomas Burdet, from Bramcote Hall, a true but sorry tale.

Other ancient buildings remaining are a tithe barn, a dove-cote, a few cottages, the Nethersole Centre which originally was a school, and the Nunnery Gateway, which is the entrance way to the church. Yes, long ago there were nuns in Polesworth and they taught needlework to the girls of the village. In the 17th century Sir Francis Nethersole founded a school so that boys and girls would have a free education.

The lovely thatched house in the Square which was a landmark, the flour mill by the river and Little Jim's Cottage have long since gone. There is a poem in print about 'Little Jim' the collier's son.

Polesworth was one of the first villages to have electricity, a luxury indeed if only for lighting. It was generated at Pooley Hall colliery. The colliery was established by a New Zealand family named Chaytor who had purchased Pooley Hall with its lands in

123

the late 1800s. In the lawn field near the colliery, where there is a monument to the colliers who gave their lives in the First World War, an annual gymkhana was held, and hundreds of people enjoyed this special day. The pit ponies too enjoyed it because they came up for an airing and a welcome graze.

The canal winds its way through Polesworth and years ago the local firm of Lees & Atkins built and repaired long boats at Polesworth docks. One member of the firm who painted the lovely roses and castles is alive today.

The winters of long ago were very severe, and most people could skate. They would skate by moonlight on the frozen canal, and if there wasn't a moon they lit candles and placed them on either side. Villagers formed their own concert party and morris dancing troupe and there seemed to be as many pubs as villagers. In fact, there is one pub less today and the population is approximately 8,000. There was a cinema for them to enjoy, even if it was converted from a flour mill, and to get them there regularly, a serial was always included.

With the closure of the colliery and clay works, which had chimneys that belched out the most fearful smoke and sulphur fumes, most people today have to commute to nearby towns and cities. But now that the M42 is open, and a section of it runs through the parish, life has been made easier for commuters.

In a lovely setting near the river is the park, a legacy one could say from the Second World War, for during that time Park Farm was commandeered for open-cast coal mining, and afterwards the site was transformed into a park for the people.

Preston Bagot ✍

Preston Bagot, just to the east of Henley-in-Arden is a small village with an interesting little church.

The church of All Saints stands high on a hill. It is very peaceful there and the churchyard is kept with loving care. Those who are lucky enough to be there at the right moment may see the altar cross set ablaze with light, the architect having designed the window so that at sunset the dying sun strikes directly upon the cross.

The church is 11th to 12th century and is steeped in history. Upon investigation for damp many years ago, two skeletons were found between the outer and inner walls and, after considerable interest and research, were duly given a Christian burial.

Travellers are rewarded after making the steep climb up the narrow church path, with panoramic views in all directions and with the crystal clear air of this high vantage point.

Preston-on-Stour 🌿

Preston appears in most of the guide books on Warwickshire and words like 'idyllic, tranquil, picturesque, quiet backwater' are always quoted and are absolutely true. But Preston is more than that, it is a living community and has not yet become just a commuter village. It is part of Alscot Estate, and has been in the West family since 1749. Even today most houses and much of the surrounding countryside belong to the present owner, Captain James West.

The village has a population of just over 100, and a varied cross section of people live here, farmers and farm workers, local craftsmen, past and present employees of the Estate, as well as a smattering of teachers, civil servants, solicitors, retired folk and young mothers. Preston is said to derive its name from 'Priestown', and Alscot Park (the West family mansion) is built on the foundations of an ancient monastery belonging to Deerhurst Priory. The oldest house in the village, whose angle completely defies gravity, is still called the Priest's House, and was said to have been used by the monks conducting services in the church of St Mary.

Take the turning to Preston after crossing the Stour and you find yourself in The Street, with its neat Victorian brick houses on either side, quite a model village in the early 1850s when they were rebuilt. Each has its own outhouse or 'brewhouse' and pig sty at the back, and a yew tree by the front gate. This old tradition is rarely seen these days, and so Preston is rightly proud of its yew trees, the symbol of immortal life. At the end of The Street is the village green, with the church of St Mary on one side and Lockes Farm on the other. The latter is a marvellous old half timbered farmhouse, and is just one of the many lovely old buildings that make up the village. Indeed, there have only been three new houses built in Preston since 1852.

From the green there are two loop roads. The top one leads up past the Old Thatch to Park Farm, the bottom one past labourers cottages and The Dell to Lower Farm. Both farms are very important in the working life of the village and their activities are a constant source of interest throughout the year.

A very old tradition carried out in Preston is the Harvest Supper held in October at the Village Hall. This dates back to the time when much of the stock had to be killed before the winter months, and today it is still very much a meat meal. Between 80 and 90 villagers sit down at two long candlelit trestles to plates of cold turkey, ham and beef and enjoy a really old fashioned harvest supper with their neighbours.

One of the most delightful things about all these village functions is the age range of those attending – from the very old to the very young all join in. Talking to older members of the village, Preston has certainly changed over the years. For instance in the 1920s Alscot estate used to employ about 30 villagers working at the Park, gardens and farm land, but now that number is drastically reduced. There is no doubt that like most rural communities Preston is under threat.

Princethorpe 🦚

No, not a romantic prince, but probably an Anglo-Saxon farmer called Pren. The name has been known for 800 years.

Joseph Elkington of Stretton was awarded £1,000 by Parliament in 1795 for his new land-drainage system. Hitherto, open drains were used in the fields, despite their interference with cultivation. Elkington drained a field in Princethorpe to show how wet marginal land could be made productive – a necessary step in the Agricultural Revolution. The Government hastened with the payment in case all knowledge of his original 1764 discovery died with him as he was in 'precarious health'. From the award was founded the family firm of Elkingtons, the famous silversmiths.

126

Early this century the village was much more self-contained and self-sufficient than it is today. Men worked on their own farms and smallholdings or for other farmers including the Priory.

Ghost stories are common but strangely none of the ghosts haunted Coffin Walk between Princethorpe and the parish church at Stretton, which traditionally was maintained at five feet, ie the width of a coffin and bearers. This path forks to The Shoulder of Mutton in Stretton. Perhaps the bearers came back that way!

The outstanding building is the Priory church. Added by Peter Paul Pugin in 1897, its fine red brick tower is a landmark. The site was acquired by a group of French Benedictine nuns from Montargis who in 1792 escaped from the French Revolution, helped by Mrs Fitzherbert, the Prince Regent's wife. The nuns had been forced by a bad storm to land at Shoreham and the Prince himself thoughtfully sent carriages from Brighton for them. He arranged overnight lodging and ordered travelling cloaks for their journey to Norfolk where they had been lent a house. In gratitude, the nuns have ever since sung a daily prayer for the Sovereign.

After several moves, the nuns bought land at Princethorpe in 1832 and settled there in the new building with their school. The bricks were made of clay dug on site and fired nearby. A reservoir built there and later artistically landscaped to resemble a small lake at Montargis was christened Little Switzerland. The building of the Pugin church brought hundreds of sightseers every weekend to watch progress.

The Second World War saw several small factories in the village making supplies for the Forces and Civil Defence. Entertaining the Forces was both a duty and a pleasure. Caravans, spare rooms and even outhouses were crowded with Coventrians seeking relief from the nightly bombing.

The early 1950s were an exciting time in Princethorpe. Roman coins were found near Stoneyford Bridge (previous finds included an Anglo-Saxon brooch and an iron spearhead). The notorious Princethorpe bank robber was thought to have buried his loot by his house in Nun's Wood but nobody has been lucky enough to find that. The new road was made then, so that pedestrians no longer had to dodge into the refuges cut into the steep banks on either side of the old narrow Coventry–Oxford road near The

Three Horse Shoes, a defile often known as 'the Khyber Pass'.

Today most farms are private houses and none of the few holdings now worked is bigger than 65 acres. Much of the land is farmed from two large farms in neighbouring villages. Princethorpe College and the two hotels provide work for many of the women, but otherwise Princethorpe is now a dormitory village even though many of the old families still live there.

Priors Hardwick

In common with many ancient villages Hardwick's beginnings remain obscure. It can, however, be said with certainty that Hardwick in the Hundred of Honesberie was one of 24 vills with which Earl Leofric endowed the monastery which he founded in Coventry sometime before 1043. Hardwick is also recorded in the Domesday Book.

Sometime before the Dissolution of the Monasteries the village was destroyed, with subsequent depopulation. The destruction was probably ordered by the Prior of Coventry to provide solitude for the monks and grazing for the flocks of sheep introduced to cater for the wool and meat markets. The site of the deserted village lies behind St Mary's church in the field known as Farm Close. The fishponds are still discernible together with several house platforms and a number of holloways.

After the Dissolution of the Monasteries Sir Edmund and Lady Ursula Knightley were granted the manor. Repopulation began in the late 16th century on the fringes of the former village.

There were at least 20 holders of lands in the parish at this time. They farmed in the open fields, growing barley, oats, wheat, peas, hay and hops, and grazing cattle, horses and sheep. That the Rainbows, Wilkshiers, Gubbins, Sherleys and their neighbours must have worked hard to survive on the heavy clay soil goes without saying. How they took their leisure, if indeed they had any, remains to be discovered.

Spice must surely have been added to life in the village by the visits of the, by all accounts, lively Welsh drovers as they progressed on their way to and from the London markets with their herds

128

of cattle, sheep, pigs or flocks of geese. The ancient Salt Road, used for carrying salt and other commodities from Droitwich to Northampton would doubtless have brought travellers into the settlement.

The old system of open field farming was brought to an end in 1767 with an Act of Parliament dividing and enclosing the land. With the planting of quickthorn hedges to enclose the various parcels of land the present pattern of fields began to take shape. From 1869 on into the early 1900s several small farms were sold, and acquired by one family, marking the beginning of the trend which eventually led to the amalgamation of the majority of land in the parish to form three farms.

One can imagine the effect on the community of the murder of Betsy Handcock. On the night of the 13th November 1872 she was stabbed by her husband, the local pig butcher. Edward Handcock earned himself the dubious distinction of being the last man hung in Warwick Jail.

About 172 people now live in the village. The school closed in 1959, the children now depart daily by bus or car to be educated in other places. The vicarage has been sold, the vicar now resides in Priors Marston. The village has no shop, although there is a post office, a pub with restaurant, and the beautiful old church of St Mary's. Residents see Hardwick as a tranquil place in which to live, far removed from urban activity, providing solitude without isolation. In 1988 only a handful of people find a livelihood in the community, incomes are earned in the surrounding towns, but in an everchanging world today sheep still graze in Priors Hardwick.

Priors Marston

Priors Marston lies to the south-east of the county with the village set at the side of a ridge which forms the edge of the Northamptonshire uplands. Fine views to the west can be obtained, with the Malvern Hills in the distance and on very clear days one can see as far as the Cambrian mountains.

The name Priors Marston is from the Anglo-Saxon 'merse'

meaning marsh with 'ton' meaning town (or, in this case, village). The Priors was added by the monks of the Benedictine Priory of Coventry after the manor was endowed to them, with 23 others, by Earl Leofric in 1043. It is mentioned in the Domesday Book of 1086 as part of Priors Hardwick, the next parish, but by 1236 was listed on the Priors Terriers as a separate place. However, a settlement was undoubtedly in existence many generations before these dates.

It is set on the very ancient Ridgeway Track with the Jurassic Way nearby. Priors Marston is also situated on the Droitwich to Northampton Salt Road (mentioned in 956) along which salt was carried for tanning and meat preservation. The Welsh Drovers' Road also enters the parish. This runs from the Welsh Borders through to Barnet near London. A High Constable was stationed here to deter highwaymen, as one of the main coaching routes from Warwick to London (via Towcester) also ran through the village. The Oxford canal, opened in 1790, lay just on the boundary of the village.

The parish has been mainly agricultural for hundreds of years with the ridge and furrow method of farming still evident in places. After the dissolution of Coventry Priory in 1539 the manorship passed through several hands until it was granted to Robert, Lord Spencer in 1602 who, with succeeding Spencers, greatly influenced the character of the whole area although the Priors Marston farms were mainly let off to tenants and not actually farmed by them. The general layout of the fields was finally set by The Enclosure Act of 1758, although, with modern farming, a considerable number of hedges have been removed. Earl Spencer is still Lord of the Manor.

The village, which became a conservation area in 1972, is an attractive grouping of stone and brick houses with only minor development occurring up to 40 years ago. Since then, as with practically all other villages, infilling has occurred with varying impact on the village scene. Look out for the houses around the village green. High House was built for Earl Spencer's agent. Hillview, by the War Memorial, was once the workshop of Edward Gardner, a well-known chairman of the Cotswold tradition. Next door, with its tall central chimney, is Westover Farm,

130

once owned by a famous clockmaker called Blenco Churchill (who died in 1764). His clock faces only had one hand.

Walk along the network of blue brick paths that run through the village and note how the friendly church and churchyard form part of the village with its collection of interesting tombstones. There is one for Josiah Key (died 1711), generous local benefactor who was a locksmith to the Court of William III and Queen Anne. His house still exists in the village and a lane is named after him. Nearby you will find the tombstone to Sarah Rainbow, inscribed:

'Here lieth one bereaved of life
A sober Christian and a loving wife
Seven sons – to them a mother kind
She lived to bury three – and four were left behind.'

The oldest part of the church is 13th century, the tower was remodelled in 1720 and extensive rebuilding and renovations occurred in 1863.

Records show that a number of stone houses were built around 1650 to 1700 and it is thought that, in addition to farming, the local wool trade and the building of Banbury market and manufacturing helped the prosperity of the village. The Falcon Inn is a very old building and was a calling point for stage coaches. The Holly Bush Inn is a very old building although it has only been a public house since the turn of the century.

With a total population of around 500 the parish has a modern mix of local town commuters and retired people with very few working on the farms. Over 80 per cent of the parish is now divided into four farms.

Several buildings have now been converted into holiday lets and some houses have become second homes for town dwellers. There are no local industries, and the once brickyard is now being developed for housing.

Quinton & Admington

Quinton, originally Queans-town (in Saxon language 'Quean' meant woman), was so-called because it was in the possession of the nuns of Polesworth until the Norman Conquest, when King William granted their rights to Sir Robert Marmion and his heirs.

There is a text from Ecclesiastes Ch 12 v1–12 inscribed on a tablet on the front of the old school: 'Remember now thy Creator in the days of thy youth'. The building is now used by a youth club, but it is still in possession of the Church so long as it is used for educational purposes.

Inhabitants of Quinton numbered about 300 in 1919. There are now nearer 2,500, and a new school had to be built after the Second World War to accommodate the rapidly growing number of children. This was mainly because of the proximity of the REME Camp and the necessity of housing army personnel and civilian workers. Large areas to the south of the old school are covered with army houses, and by three large council estates.

Magdalen College, Oxford, the major landowner, has sold off most of the larger houses and cottages; many of the latter have been joined to make larger dwellings. This applies especially to Admington, which remains largely unspoiled. The Hall is still privately owned, but Quinton House was sold about 40 years ago and is now a nursing home.

Most villagers now work either in the Camp or at Stratford-upon-Avon. About 60 years ago they were employed either on farms or in the nearby market gardens. There were no cars so transport was by pony and trap or bicycle, otherwise people walked. Children played in the fields and on the roads in perfect safety, bowling hoops for miles, skipping, spinning tops, hop-scotch, ball games, marbles, etc. Fox-and-hounds over Meon Hill, especially at dusk, was tremendous fun.

A farm house, Magdalen House, is now The Gay Dog public house. The College Arms was originally owned by Magdalen College and is the only pub entitled to carry the College coat of arms.

The Village Hall, built comparatively recently, is well used for all kinds of meetings and functions.

Radford Semele

The name is thought to originate from the 'Red Ford' or the 'Reeded Ford' (possibly over the river Leam), and the name of the Norman landowner in the reign of Henry I, who was Henry de Simely. Hence, the Red (or Reeded) Ford on the land of Simely.

But there is evidence of life in the village long before the reign of Henry I. A flint hand axe and two other flints were found in 1968 – they would have belonged to ancient Britons over 30,000 years ago.

Radford Semele parish lies between Leamington Spa to the west, Offchurch to the north and the Roman Fosse Way to the east. Coins dating back to the Roman period have been found in gardens in the village, so presumably there was habitation here around AD 300. The site of a Roman villa on Pounce Hill Farm, about half a mile west of the Fosse Way, was brought to light in the 1920s.

The oldest building in the village is the church. It is probable that in medieval times the village centred around the church but sometime later, by 1600, the whole village had moved half a mile away. The reason for this is not known, but the church remains isolated from the village.

There may have been a church here before the Norman Conquest, but monks from Kenilworth Priory built, or rebuilt it, in the early 12th century. The only Norman part remaining is the south wall where the typical rubble masonry and a small window can be seen. The tower, which is possibly on older foundations, is thought to be of 15th century construction. Over the centuries the church has undergone alterations and rebuilding. The church interior, as it is seen today, is largely a result of the extensive rebuilding of 1889. Some recent refurbishing has increased the feeling of being in 'an oasis of peace and quiet' in this lovely church.

Radford Hall was probably built between 1600 and 1620, and contains some fine wood carving, dated 1622, which is believed to have been done by a travelling band of Huguenots. There remains part of an ancient wall, which may have encircled the grounds and may be older than the Hall itself. A fine postern gate, in this wall, is visible from the road. In the early 19th century, the building was rebuilt, with brick covering the original stone. The Hall has recently been converted into several dwellings.

Radford was famous in the area for its ale. This was originally 'home brewed' at Radford Hall, but proved so popular that the Thornley family built a brewery on land opposite the Hall. This flourished from 1900 until takeover and closure in 1969. The site is now occupied by a design company.

There are two thatched houses on the main road through the village near the turn to Offchurch. One of these has an unusual chimney, which divides and then rejoins, with a window in the middle. This is clearly seen on the east end of the house.

The Manor House, opposite the thatched houses, was built around 1800 and has a round tower similar to the one on Edgehill. Considerable additions were made in the late 19th century. It has been divided into four dwellings.

The White Lion, with its thatched roof, is the only pub in the village, and dates back to the 17th century. A number of clay pipes have been found on land to the south of the inn. These pipes date from 1640 to 1710, and were probably thrown on the rubbish tip from The White Lion.

The old village of Radford Semele was situated along the main turnpike road and what is now called Lewis Road. There was considerable expansion in the village after 1956. Prior to this, the population had been between 500 and 600 for over a hundred years. Today the population is around 2,500.

The canal, which passes through the parish, was begun in 1795, and opened in 1800 as the Warwick and Napton Canal. It later became part of the Grand Union Canal. The original narrow locks were widened during the modernisation programme of 1925.

The railway linking Leamington with Rugby was built in 1851, and included a fine skew arched bridge over the canal near the boundary with Offchurch. The railway track was lifted in 1967. Today this part of the railway, and the canal towpath, are popular walks for villagers.

Radway 🖎

Visitors today see in the wooded slopes of Edgehill, scene of a Civil War battle in 1642, a blend of past and present and from the top, a panorama of 12 counties. Also from the top, the Round Tower, built in 1750, watches over Radway from the spot where the king's standard was set up before the battle.

The tower's architect, Sanderson Miller, planted trees below the tower, and was also responsible for the meaningless turrets added to the once beautiful Grange. The Stoneleigh monks were the early owners of the Grange, they demolished the existing building and built the main part of the present house. A well was sunk and fish-ponds were made and stocked. John Washington was the owner during the Battle of Edgehill, great uncle to George Washington, the first President of the USA. Today the Grange still plays a part in the community life.

The parish church, dedicated to St Peter, and the Methodist chapel both celebrated a centenary in 1966. When the old church was demolished, foundations of a previous one were discovered, and the Norman period gargoyles were dug up and incorporated in the tower of the present church. The five bells in the tower are enthusiastically rung on every possible occasion.

Long ago there was a strong association with the Quakers – the old Meeting House is now a private dwelling, and a garden covers the burial ground.

Horses have always been important, in bygone days for work and transport, providing useful local employment. Blacksmith, wheelwright, carrier, saddler, all had a prominent part to play. Now there are more horses than ever before, but used for different purposes. The demand today is for sport and recreation.

An early attempt at education was a 'Dame School' under the patronage of squire and vicar in a cottage at the Grange entrance. In 1851, Charles Chambers of Ivy Lodge, built the school and in 1852 an 'excellent Reading Room', now called the Institute. He left both properties in the care of his cousin, Georgiana. Eventually some Board School regulations were incorporated, and then in 1912 the County Council took over. In 1966 progress dictated that the school be closed, and now the children travel to Tysoe and to Kineton. The school is now a house.

The village is not on any big road – it lies between the main roads from Banbury to Warwick and from Banbury to Stratford. Peace is threatened now by the M40 motorway extension, which is planned to run within a very few miles of the village.

The Round Tower at Radway, built in 1750

136

Ratley with Edgehill & Upton

Ratley was a medieval village, facing south and nestling on the edge of the Cotswolds. It was built on the old Banbury to Stratford road where the pub and the church stand (now known as Featherbow Lane). From AD 1100 to the turn of the century it changed very little due to poor transport facilities. Quarrying was its first industry and provided a livelihood for the inhabitants, while farming was carried out as a means of survival. The local stone is a lovely honey brown with blue flashes and the village keeps its character with dwellings built in this stone. The Hornton stone quarry is at Edgehill and still brings employment to the area. The cutting of the old railway line which carried ironstone by rail through Ratley to the main railway line at Fenny Compton still remains, but due to a fatal accident in 1913 the line was never completed.

Land that has been quarried is being reclaimed and planted out with trees leaving grassy areas in between to encourage wild flowers. It is designated to become a Nature Reserve. In 1971 the old part of Ratley was recognised as a Conservation village and this has helped to keep the character of the village.

A barn which belongs to the village was converted into the Village Hall in 1937. Previously it had been used as a corn and potato store for the villagers and at one time as a soup kitchen for the very poor. It is now well used for recreational and educational purposes.

The local, The Rose and Crown, was a 'spit and sawdust' pub – one room with beer sold out of a jug until the 1970s, when it was transformed into a modern pub with brasses, beams, open hearth and a restaurant. It is a listed building.

Next door is the old church which in recent years has enjoyed a musical revival with musical events including performances of Handel's *Messiah*. The church has four bells. The first bell was put in in 1677, a tenor bell in 1763, a treble in 1859 and another treble in 1985. Amos John England, now living in a cottage called 'Wayside', followed his grandfather as bellringer and is, according to a previous rector, 'an astonishing one-man act on 3 ropes, pulling with both hands and one foot'.

The village school was built in 1887 but closed in 1976 due to small numbers of children in the village and high costs. The children now travel to Tysoe school, approximately 3 miles away.

Edgehill comes within the Parish boundary and is famous for past events, but mostly for the Civil War battle of 1642, fought underneath the escarpment in the Parish of Radway. Ghost legends and myths of the battle still persist, such as sounds of battle, and sightings of the galloping white charger said to be Prince Rupert's.

Upton House stands a mile away from Edgehill and was built in the 17th century. It is now a National Trust property and brings many visitors and tourists to our village and woods. In the summer there is a typical English scene of white clad figures on the cricket pitch, and in the winter the Warwickshire hunt hold their meet at the House.

Rowington 🌿

Anybody looking for the village of Rowington has a difficult task, for it is a place of scattered hamlets originally established by a group of Saxons of Hwicce heritage. Their leader was 'Hroca' and their settlement 'Hrocingatun', meaning 'homestead of Hroca's people'. In the Domesday Book this had become 'Rochintone'. The whole area was then covered by part of the Forest of Arden, and thus a typical fragmented woodland village was formed, which is now bisected by the B4439 road to Warwick.

There remain some substantial heavily timbered old houses in the parish, and Shakespeare Hall is one which must be mentioned. Legend has it that a branch of the Shakespeare family lived here in William Shakespeare's time, and there is ample evidence of Shakespeare farmers in the community for many years. Whether or not they were directly connected with the famous bard remains a mystery!

The nearby quarry, now extinct, was once of considerable importance. Rowington stone was used extensively in Warwickshire buildings, notably for St Philip's cathedral, Birmingham, for

Baddesley Clinton Hall (NT) and, of course, for the parish church of St Lawrence.

The village has a strong association with windmills. Long-term residents remember 'Bouncing Bessie' in action. Mr Boyle was in charge – and permanently covered in flour, we are told! 'Grinning Jenny' is believed to have been a wooden post mill; and 'Tom o'the Wood' was apparently near to the Tom o'the Wood Inn, renamed in 1975 for this reason.

The Wilson family of Shakespeare Hall were among several benefactors of this century, and gave the land on which the Village Hall now stands. Mr E. L. Edwards was another. In 1912 he purchased the nearby field used for cricket and rented it to the club for a nominal sum. Forty years later, in 1952, his two daughters gave the ground to the village in trust. Mr and Mrs F. S. Ryland (also one-time owners of Shakespeare Hall) added to the amenities by funding the adjacent Rowington Working Men's Club.

Before the existence of the Village Hall, the school was the hub of social as well as educational activity, thanks to its public-

The Cock Horse Inn, Rowington

spirited headmaster, Mr Herbert McWilliams. Fetes and concert parties were his passions – the Nondescript Concert Party Group particularly, which provided great village entertainment. The demise of his school, from 100 pupils down to a tiny handful when it closed in 1984, would have been unthinkable to Mr McWilliams, and was a sad day for everyone!

At The Cock Horse inn the unforgettable Maud Barlow succeeded her father and grandfather as landlord. The Cock was also the forge, and her father was blacksmith as well as landlord! Large in every sense, Maud is pictured in the Public Bar on a winter's evening in front of a roaring fire (which nearly singed the coat of her old dog), where she entertained all comers. Known far and wide, the story goes that a local resident on holiday abroad, mentioned to some Americans that he lived in Warwickshire, whereupon they immediately inquired whether he knew Maud Barlow at The Cock inn!

Today the little shops, the Cobbler's Hut and the Woodsheds near the schoolhouse have gone, yet Rowington is fortunate in that the surrounding Green Belt has saved it from large-scale development. Some residents commute to nearby towns, but painters, decorators, builders, gardeners and nurserymen find employment locally, and there are still a number of working farms. There is even a working shepherd!

Nevertheless, change continues. The Rector is in charge now of the five Parishes of the North Ferncumbe Group to which Rowington belongs, and by 1989 there will be the M40 between the village and Lowsonford! This is the third time in recent history that this peaceful valley has suffered invasion – first by the canal, then by the railway line, and now by a six-lane motorway!

Salford Priors 🖋️

The village lies on the main road between Stratford-upon-Avon and Evesham. Coming over Marridge Hill (many years ago called Marl Ridge) you see to the left the river Arrow gently making its way through the fields to where it joins the Avon. To the right can be seen the hamlet of Dunnington, and straight ahead the tower of the parish church can just be seen through the surrounding trees, a peaceful and pleasant view. The Parish consists of the village of Salford Priors with the hamlets of Abbots Salford, Rushford, Irons Cross, Cock Bevington, Wood Bevington and Dunnington.

It is a very old village going back to Saxon times and there are still 13 black and white thatched cottages. The old village name was Salteford Major, with Abbots Salford being Salteford Minor, as they were on the Salt Way from Droitwich. St Mary's Priory Kenilworth came into possession of the village, so it became Priors Salford. Salteford Minor passed into the hands of the Abbot of Evesham and so became Abbots Salford.

The church of St Matthew stands surrounded by fields, said to have grown grapes in the days of the Romans. At the entrance to the church is a lovely Norman doorway, built about 1080. There are Norman arches inside from when the church was extended, lancet windows of the 13th century, and a beautiful Flamboyant window.

One of the most celebrated inhabitants was Valentine Green. Born in 1739, he became a mezzotint engraver to King George III and was also commissioned by the Elector of Bavaria.

Another inhabitant who left his mark was William Perkins who was a tailor. Believing in education, he left money for this purpose, and eventually a shcool was built in 1860, which is still used and has been extended. In 1900 scholarships were awarded through the Perkins Trust to the Grammar School, this continuing until 1948. The Trust still continues for the benefit of the young people of the area.

In Abbots Salford stands a beautiful building, Salford Hall, now undergoing renovation to be used as a hotel. At one time it belonged to John Alderford, whose daughter Margaret married Sir Simon Clark in the 17th century. She died, and there is a large heraldic memorial erected in 1631 to her memory. He later married Lady Dorothy Hay who was the daughter of Thomas Hobson of Cambridge, the carrier and stage coach owner, who became famous for the expression 'Hobson's Choice'. There is a beautiful and unusual memorial to Lady Dorothy in the church. The Hall was also used by nuns from 1807 until 1838, where they started a school for young ladies, and until recent years the house was always referred to as the Nunnery by the local people.

Until the Second World War the parish was self-supporting as there was a wheelwright and carpenter (who was also the undertaker), a blacksmith, cobbler, baker, and dairy farmer. The main occupation for the men was in agriculture, until an engineering works was started by Bomford Bros at Pitchill. The firm of Bomford and Evershed has now expanded to a modern factory beside the Banbrook, where agricultural machinery is exported all over the Continent, and provides employment for many people.

Park Hall, a lovely old house and grounds now being made into flats and dwelling houses, was the Dower House to Ragley Hall. The present Marquis was born here when his parents Lord and Lady Henry Seymour were in residence.

Going up to the Bevingtons, the views are breathtaking. There is an old manor house at Wood Bevington and at Dunnington there is a school built like a small church. Indeed it was used as a school all the week and a church on Sundays until after the Second World War, now it is just the Primary School. There is also a very nice Baptist church standing in the middle of the hamlet with once again beautiful views over the surrounding lands.

Sambourne ✑

Sambourne has been a community for 900 years. Drovers met at 'Sandburne' before making the journey through the ancient forest of Feckenham. In the recent past, small industries, connected with needle making, were based in Sambourne. These, along with a forge, a mill and a small brick kiln, have now disappeared.

Today, Sambourne is a rural community of some 150 houses and 350 inhabitants, surrounded by attractive countryside. It is a peaceful village and although it is close to both Redditch and Studley, it has succeeded in maintaining its identity.

The social centre of the village, if not the geographical centre, is the village green with its war memorial and chestnut trees. The village green is used by the community for village functions and the main 'village' buildings are found here.

The pub is next to the green. The present building, flanked by yew trees, is over 400 years old and replaced an earlier inn. It is a black and white timber-framed structure. Inside, original oak beams and stone floors are welcoming. On the opposite side of the green is the building which housed the village shop and post office. Sadly, like so many other village shops, this has now closed and Sambourne has lost an important meeting place.

Sambourne is part of the widespread parish of Coughton, Sambourne, Spernal, Morton Bagot and Oldberrow. As such, Sambourne does not have a parish church, this being at Coughton. Instead it has a building next to the green which is used for both worship and village meetings. In 1982, villagers raised money to build a meeting place for Sambourne. An area was separated from the main room by a screen. This area stores the lectern and table so that when the screen is removed the room can be used for church services. The building was opened with a service followed by tea and entertainment. Thus, the joint function of the building was established and Sambourne can be proud that past residents built such a useful building.

Houses in Sambourne are a pleasing blend of old and new. Most are situated to the north-west of the green. There are several old, part-timbered houses including Yew Tree Cottage (the green) and Crossroads (Sambourne Lane). An attractive terrace of cottages on Sambourne Lane is maintained by the Sambourne Trust, a village charity dedicated to the welfare of villagers.

The population of Sambourne is made up of a broad spectrum of people. Some families can claim to have lived in the village for generations. Others are newcomers. Various village organisations, the church, the WI, the Parish Council and hopefully, in the future, a 'community society', draw the community together.

Seckington ❧

A very small hamlet with a population of 47, Seckington possesses a disproportionate wealth of history.

In AD 757 King Ethelbald of Mercia (and ruler of all England

Seckington Church

south of the Humber) was killed here, either murdered by his own thanes or killed in battle by his successor, Beornred.

The well-preserved motte and bailey, a tree-covered mound easily seen from the A453, is a later defence, probably Norman.

Seckington appears in the Domesday Book. The Manor was held by the Burdett family from the time of Henry II (reigned 1154–1189), and passed down in the direct male line from Edward III's reign (1327–1377) until 1919. The church contains a fine Elizabethan monument to Robert Burdett (died 1603) and his wife. It also depicts their two sons and two daughters. In 1316 a Robert Burdett held the Manor jointly with Gerald de Sekyndon, whose descendants, now called Seckington (like the village), still maintain connections with the village of their ancestors.

Another family of interest was the Washington family who owned and occupied two properties here during the reign of Henry VIII. Sycamore Cottage, although rebuilt, is thought to have been one of these. George Washington, first President of the United States, was a descendant of these Washingtons. His great-grandfather, John Washington, settled in Virginia in 1657 and may have been from Seckington. The coat of arms of the family used to be in the church.

The present village is principally a farming community consisting of four old farms (three working), farm cottages, a Victorian Gothic Old Rectory and a small number of modern houses.

Shottery

Many people hearing the name Shottery would inevitably think of Shakespeare and without question the Bard has had a great deal to do with the present popularity of Shottery – a 'must' on the visitors' lists. But the history of Shottery goes much further back than the 16th century when Shakespeare was born. Among the earliest relics to have been found here are fossils of the skeletons of echinoderms – plant-like invertebrates – which may be seen in the museum at New Place (Nash's House). Also in the museum is a collection of Middle Stone Age flints dating from 8000–3500 BC.

There is also evidence that the Romans came to Shottery, as three Roman coins were found at the foot of Bordon Hill, and the Alcester Road is also part of a Roman road.

Shottery is featured in Domesday Book and in 1182 accounted for an acreage of approximately 800 acres which would support about 70 people. By the late medieval period there were two great houses in Shottery. The Manor House, now Shottery Girls' Grammar School on the east side of Shottery Brook and The Hewlands, a large farmhouse later to be known as Ann Hathaway's Cottage on the west. The houses in tavern Lane were associated with the Manor House and those in the Hamlet with The Hewlands.

There were a number of housing developments in the 1930s and since the end of the Second World War extensive building developments have been made.

In the field of education, it seems there was a Dame School provided by a charity founded by Thomas Eden of Weston-sub-Edge in 1733 for 21 boys and girls aged 5–9 years. They were to be taught spelling, reading, to recite the Catechism and sewing for the girls. For this the Dame was paid £9.2s. a year. Books, Bibles and Testaments were provided by the charity. When the Education Act of 1870 was passed, this amount of schooling was considered inadequate and a new school was built – the actual building being a tithe barn transported from Redditch, donated by the Rev A. H. Williams of Alcester. The school was opened on 2nd December 1870.

Until 1871, it is assumed that Shottery villagers worshipped at Holy Trinity, the parish church of Stratford. There was a Nonconformist chapel near The Bell Inn from about 1833. This is now the Elim Pentecostal church. In 1870 land was given by the Priest in Charge at Bishopton church for the building of a church at Shottery.

After the end of the Second World War a Memorial Hall was built in Hathaway Lane, and this serves as a venue for many and varied activities and organisations. One of these is a Women's Institute market which meets on Friday mornings where an excellent selection of high quality produce is on sale.

At the end one must return to Shakespeare. It is his fame which has brought Shottery world wide recognition and many thousands of visitors, including Royalty and Heads of State, every year to visit Ann Hathaway's Cottage, now in the care of the Shakespeare Birthplace Trust. Cottages built near to Ann Hathaway's Cottage have been improved in recent times and their colourful gardens contribute a floral welcome, while nearby tearooms and restaurants provide sustenance and cheer before the visitors return to their hotels or homes.

Shrewley, Little Shrewley, Hatton & Haseley ✤

On the fringe of Shakespeare country, in the heart of England (very few places could be further from the nearest sea) lie the Warwickshire villages of Shrewley, Little Shrewley, Hatton and Haseley.

Little Shrewley, nowadays just a hamlet of attractive old and new houses, was once the hub of the area, with a pin factory, grinding mill and large nursery garden, all of which ceased functioning as such before the Second World War. Although the pin factory and nursery, as well as a fair-sized coal yard, have disappeared, the mill has reopened within the last four years as a craft centre, specialising in pine furniture and bookbinding.

A local character of Little Shrewley (or just Shrewley as it was then known) was one farmer 'Jampot' Taylor who kept all his money in a jam jar – presumably well-hidden – while his two spinster sisters kept theirs in body belts. The hitching up of layers of petticoats, not to mention corsets and liberty bodices, whenever ready cash was called for must have been a sight to behold – waiting local tradesmen must have had a field day!

Shrewley Common, merely an area of open land in Little Shrewley's heyday, is part of the benefice with Hatton and Haseley. It has an Independent chapel, a hairdresser (who takes dry-cleaning as well), and a most excellent family-run post office and store. This caters for the holiday craft on the canal which runs, via a long tunnel, under the village street. At the west end of the street is The Durham Ox – a popular 17th century free house inn. In the 1950s a circus had its winter quarters ¾ mile beyond Shrewley and the long straight road through the village was ideal for the daily exercising of the performing elephants. The elephant walk was regarded with amused indulgence by the villagers except, probably, Mr Hobley, who had a bread round and, having left the van door open, the entire contents were consumed, with apparent relish, by the appreciative animals. What the erstwhile policeman, Sergeant Puddyfoot, would have said is not hard to imagine.

Shrewley boasts a flourishing marina on the Grand Union Canal alongside Hatton Station. A well-known landmark is the Hatton flight of 21 locks on the canal along a stretch of 2¼ miles up Hatton Hill, where intrepid boatmen can slake their thirsts at The Waterman Inn at the top.

Hatton has a comprehensive and busy craft centre with a pick-your-own fruit and vegetable area, and a most attractive cafe.

The A41 main road runs past Hatton church, with its 16th century tower. Haseley's beautiful small church is indeed old. There was known to be a Saxon chapel on the site and the nave is almost certainly Norman, the chancel is 13th century and the tower was added in the 15th century. The tomb of Clement Throckmorton, who died in 1573, lies in a square bay on the south side of the church. During recent renovations a section of wall revealed some religious medieval paintings. Running immediately outside Shrewley Common is the M40 motorway, well under construction with junction access less than 4 miles from the village, straight to the Capital itself.

Although so very near to all this progress, the villages are completely surrounded by countryside with pleasant views, some pastoral, some quite dramatic as from the top of Hatton Hill.

Shustoke ❧

The village of Shustoke covers just over 2,000 acres, and the population is in the region of 500 people. It lies about 3 miles from Coleshill, on the Nuneaton road.

It is a rural area, with quite a number of farms, a large amount of the land and property belonging to Sir William Dugdale of Blyth Hall (also of Merevale Hall, Atherstone).

Shustoke is mentioned in the Domesday Book as Scotscote, and there are numerous other spellings in old documents and records.

The parish church of St Cuthbert lies about 1 mile above the village. There was a church in Saxon times, later replaced by a more substantial building of the Norman period, and again a further replacement in the 14th century, which was later completely altered in the Victorian era. That church was irreparably damaged by a fire after having been struck by lightning in 1886, and 1987 saw the centenary of its restoration. The most famous feature of the church is undoubtedly the tomb of the renowned antiquary, Sir William Dugdale, ancestor of the present Sir William and author of *The Antiquities of Warwickshire*. He was born at what is now known as 'The Old Rectory' in Shawbury Lane.

Near to the church are 5 almshouses, part of the cottages being on the site of the former village school. These are administered under the Huntbach Trust. Until the Plague in 1650, the village was situated near to the church, but people then moved away and built dwellings which formed the nucleus of the present village.

The local school became a First School in 1987, taking children up to the age of 8, not only from Shustoke but from the surrounding villages. It is situated in a very pleasant spot.

The local pub, The Plough, is nearby, and in addition to the regulars one may on occasion see a group of ramblers who have come out to Shustoke for a breath of fresh air and a bit of healthy exercise.

Next to the pub is the Village Pound in which sheep were penned ready for collection for market years ago, and any stray animals were shut in there awaiting collection by their owners. The structure of the Pound was restored by the Parish Council in 1975.

There is a local post office & stores (built about 1470), where, in addition to having a friendly chat with the proprietor, one may also purchase almost any commodity one could name.

Not far from the village centre is Shustoke Reservoir which, with the reservoir in the adjoining parish of Whitacre, and Whitacre Water Works, supplies water to bulk storage reservoirs at

Coventry and Nuneaton. There is an enthusiastic sailing club which is based at the reservoir, and anglers also spend many happy hours sitting on the banks fishing for trout.

Shuttington ✍

Shuttington is a small residential village of mainly 19th and 20th century buildings, standing high on a hill overlooking Alvecote Pools Nature Reserve. It has more ancient origins however: it was mentioned in the Domesday survey, and the little Norman church was once a chapel to Alvecote Priory.

In the churchyard is buried an 18th century record breaker! Thomas Spooner was the fattest man in England, weighing 40 stone 9 lbs, and measuring 4 feet 3 inches across the shoulders. Such was his size that he could only get around by pony and trap, but his bulk saved his life when, during an argument, he was stabbed and his fat prevented the wound being fatal.

The public house, The Wolferstan Arms is named after the landowning family of nearby Statfold Hall.

The former Working Men's Club is now Shuttington Craft Centre, and there is also a village shop and a riding school.

Community spirit is strong in the village, which is raising the funds to build a village hall.

Snitterfield ✍

The village lies halfway between Stratford-upon-Avon and Warwick. Its origins are obscure but there is thought to have been a settlement as early as Celtic times, and certainly by the time of the Domesday Book there was a flourishing community. The earliest recorded name was Snytenfeld (in Anglo Saxon 'place of snipe') because the bottom lands of the village, now drained by the Sherborne Brook, were at one time the haunt of snipe, being very boggy. They still are in wet weather, but alas the snipe have gone although there are still herons, and reputedly kingfishers, though the latter are rarely seen. The name was corrupted to Snitfeld and later to its present form.

The village used to be the centre of a thriving agricultural community, with several large farms and most of the villagers employed in farmwork and allied crafts. Gradually the way of life altered until the Second World War saw the end of the varied trades, such as hurdlemaker, blacksmith, saddler and wheelwright which had formerly made the village a self-sufficient farming enclave.

There was even, during the Victorian era, a village brick-kiln and local bricks were extensively used when the Philips family, who virtually owned the village for 100 years from 1816, rebuilt or improved many of the houses.

Today, with modern transport, the neighbouring towns of Stratford-upon-Avon and Warwick are so easily accessible that there is no longer the need for local facilities. Sadly, where there were at one time four or five shops, the last remaining one closed down in 1987. Fortunately there is still the post-office, and even more fortunately, the doctors' surgery and dispensary.

Probably the most famous farmer in local history was Richard Shakespeare, the grandfather of the Bard, who farmed land near the church which he rented from John Arden of Wilmcote, whose daughter Mary married Richard's son John. If only they had stayed here instead of moving to Stratford shortly before William's birth, what a different village this might have become. As it was, the farm was carried on by a ne'er-do-well brother Henry (known to William Shakespeare as 'Uncle Harry') who appears to have been a sore trial both to his father and to his more prosperous brother John.

There is an early Tudor house still standing just beyond the church which is claimed by some to have been the Shakespeare house but this is not certain, and from contemporary records it seems more likely to have been in a different part of the village, probably demolished long ago. There are, however, still a number of genuine Tudor houses remaining in the village, most in private occupation and in better repair than the alleged Shakespeare house. One of them has the additional interest of a ghost! This is reputed to be the shade of a soldier, mortally wounded at the Civil

War battle of Edgehill who managed to make his way to Snitterfield, but died in the house.

Apart from the Tudor and Jacobean architecture there are two other main types of houses in the village – the Philips houses referred to earlier, which are all in the same distinctive brick and stone style, and many post-war houses, including a fairly extensive council estate.

The recent completion of the Stratford Northern By-pass, which runs right across the southern edge of the village not only destroyed the beautiful tree-lined road known as Kings Lane, (because Prince Charles, later King Charles II, is reputed to have fled along it when escaping after his defeat at Worcester) but seems likely to alter the nature of the village even more when it links up with the M40 extension.

Southam

Although there is no documentary evidence relating to Southam before AD 998, Roman coins discovered during the 19th century in the churchyard and Bury Orchard indicate the probability of a Roman settlement around AD 250–350.

The first documentation is a Charter of King Ethelred the Unready which gave Southam to Leofwine, father of Leofric (husband of Lady Godiva) in 998. Southam is also recorded in the Domesday Book of 1086. The ownership of Southam passed from Leofwine to his son, who bestowed it upon the Prior of Coventry in 1047.

Southam's chief claim to historical fame rests in events immediately prior to the Civil War in 1641, when Charles I is said to have passed through the town. Apparently he was not made welcome and the churchwardens refused to ring the bells. The furious king had the church doors locked until they paid a fine of 13 shillings and 4 pence. However, the stubborn bellringers still refused to ring the bells to wish him 'Godspeed' on his departure, so he sent his footmen back to levy another fine of 5 shillings.

King Charles later returned to Southam and is said to have slept at the Manor House on Market Hill before the Battle of Edgehill. Not to be outdone, the Roundheads also came to the town, and

Cromwell himself was here in 1645 with 7,000 troops. However, although battles raged nearby, Southam was not again to become involved in the fighting.

Until the year 1820 four annual fairs took place in Southam. The most important was the Charter Fair, established in 1257 to be held on the Vigil Feast and morrow of St Peter and St Paul. By far the most popular fair was the 'Show Fair' held on the Monday of the first week in June. This included a Lady Godiva Procession probably to commemorate the handing of Southam by Leofric and Lady Godiva to the Monks of Coventry.

St James' parish church was built in perpendicular style in the 16th century. In the tower there is a peal of eight bells. The pulpit is late 16th century.

In 1818 Mr Henry Tilley Smith established an infirmary for eye and ear disorders. The dispensary cottage dated 1840 is no longer in existence but a stone surmounted by an urn is situated near the site, in front of The Stoneythorpe Hotel on the Warwick road, to commemorate the first Provident Dispensary in the country.

The Holywell, according to Arthur Mee's *Warwickshire* is 'Holywell that never freezes and a street that always pleases'. It is thought that the waters from the well were regarded as a cure for eye ailments.

Stockingford 🦜

Stokeyingford, Stokeford or Stooking Lane are names given to land which has been enclosed from wild land since medieval times. The word 'stocking' means stocking up of woodlands or wastelands, and preparing for cultivation. The area which embraces Stockingford at one time was part of the Forest of Arden.

The word 'Ford' means a stream and such a ford existed from a short distance beyond Stockingford station.

A site in Stockingford with woodlands and arable land was granted in 1143 by Earl Robert le Bossn and William de Newmarch to the Canons of St Mary de Pre of Leicester. The Canons had a chapel here by grant of Geoffrey de Turville. The Manor of Stockingfold may be identified with these messuages, and a mill and other land were granted in 1280 by Hugh de Lilleburn to his son Hugh.

In 1898 several acres of glebe land were sold, and as there was a demand for housing accommodation building began in Church Road and Haunchwood Road. The allotment association was formed and provided 360 allotments. St Paul's church was built on Paddiford Common and consecrated in 1824.

In 1904 oil lamps were discarded and gas lighting was put in. The church was the first public building in England to be lit with the inverted gas mantles.

The main industries in Stockingford were the coal mines and brickyards, which sadly are now all closed, also the Stockingford railway station. In 1887 another pit was working in the Chapel End district which was then included in the Stockingford parish. This pit was termed 'Drybread' on account of the poor pay of the miners.

The Round Towers are north of Arbury Hall and the southern end of Church Road and form the main entrance to Arbury Hall. They are in fine preservation and built of local stone. There is an embattled gateway on either side of which are the residences of the two gatekeepers.

Mary Ann Evans (George Eliot) was born at South Farm on the Arbury Estate. A bronze statue of her was made at the nearby studio of John Letts of Astley, and placed in Newdigate Square in Nuneaton town centre in 1986.

The last Monday in June was a big day in Stockingford. The church and chapels held their Sunday School treats. St Paul's church processed round the parish with banners and bunting and singing hymns. After tea in the church school, games and races were held in Mr Burdett's field, and every child was given a penny bun. The local brass band headed the procession and played music in the field at night.

Stockton ✿

The first mention of Stockton, which means 'Stump Enclosure', appears in records dated 1272.

It remained a tiny farming hamlet until the discovery of clay and lime in the vicinity. The development of cement and lime industries in the 18th and 19th centuries has had the most influence on the village. Housing was provided for employees and the village increased in numbers.

The industry was sold to Nelson Cement Works early in the 19th century. With the profits the church was renovated and the remaining money was used to employ a Church of England school teacher. A stone house, originally a stable, served as a schoolroom for the local children. By 1824, 33 boys and 19 girls were benefiting from an education. The present day school was built in 1906 and is still in use today as a 'first' school.

During the excavation of the blue lias pit just outside Stockton in 1898, an almost perfect fossil of an ichthyosaurus was found 30 feet below the surface. It lay flat, face down with its paddles spread either side of its body and tail curved to the side, length 19 feet 5 inches. Its age is estimated at 20 million years. The dinosaur was carefully removed and could until recently be seen in the Natural History Museum.

At the turn of this century a rector took up the living in Stockton and his eccentric behaviour is still a topic of conversation today. Archdeacon Colley, as he insisted on being called, although the title had lapsed when he retired from an archdeaconate in the South African diocese of Natal, could be seen wearing his mitre and gown at all times. To encourage children to attend services Archdeacon Colley would play a cornet at the gate of the church each Sunday and in the front pew he had installed a dulcimer for them to play during the hymns.

Perhaps the most unusual act performed by this eccentric rector was the building of his own glass topped coffin. The coffin was kept for many years in his study in the rectory where the children preparing for confirmation would use it as a seat.

A real character of the village was Mr Charles Gardner, well-known all over the world for his wood turning. His first lathe was improvised from an old treadle sewing machine and a car gear box.

Accompanied by his wife, he began to attend the Royal Shows. Invitations followed to attend fairs all over the country, Ireland

and Scotland included. It was at the Royal Show that he met many members of the Royal family, including the Queen Mother, Princess Anne and Princess Alexandra. An elephant carved for the Duke of Gloucester's collection, a salad bowl for Princess Alexandra and egg cups for her children were among his royal commissions. Field-Marshal Montgomery received a cheese platter made by Mr Gardner.

The types of wood used were of great significance to Mr Gardner. He knew the origins and type of each piece, many pieces coming from his own garden. His famous model fair roundabout embodies 78 varieties of wood.

Master craftsman Neville Neal, born and bred in Stockton, has been working with wood since he left school at the age of 14. Now, nearly half a century later, his graceful cottage chairs with their slender legs, tall ladder backs and comfortable rush seats are in great demand all over the world. The rushes are collected at the end of July from the upper river Leam near Leamington Hastings, they are then hung to dry to last through the winter. The ash wood used is especially chosen from local timber.

Stoneleigh

Stoneleigh is steeped in history – a thousand years of development on the banks of the river Sowe which is crossed by Rennie's beautiful bridge of eight arches built in the 19th century. Stoneleigh Abbey is situated in parkland one mile south of the village across fields which now form the Royal Showground.

Stanlei, as it was called once, lay deep in the Forest of Arden. Now some great oaks still standing in the park are all that remain. Stoneleigh was a royal manor until the reign of Henry I, with its own Hundred Court on Motslow Hill, named from 'moot' or meeting place. Its quarry provided the stone for the church and almshouses.

Through the centuries the village reflected changing times and fortunes. By the time of the Domesday Survey, the manor possessed two mills and 4 miles of woodland in which the king owned the feeding for 2,000 hogs. Later, the living was given to the monks of Kenilworth until the Reformation.

In 1561, Sir Thomas Leigh, Lord Mayor of London, who rode before Elizabeth to her coronation, bought the estate from the Crown. His daughter, Alice, who survived him, married Sir Robert Dudley, illegitimate son of the Queen's favourite, Earl of Leicester. He spent many years trying to prove the legitimacy of his birth but without success. An embittered man, he went to Italy with Elizabeth Southwell – maid of honour to the Queen. Meanwhile Alice, who was created a Duchess in her own right in 1644, was left with her four daughters to administer her estates. She consoled herself by helping the poor and needy. She built the almshouses with their quaint roofs and double rows of high chimneys.

The village changed little over the next four centuries with the Norman church, famous for its Romanesque chancel arch and apostle font, in the meadows by the river, the Parsonage close by. The smithy, still in use today, stood on the green beside a spreading chestnut tree. A handsome Elizabethan manor house stands proudly overlooking the church meadows where cattle still graze. The school, which was converted from the courthouse, closed in 1975 and has now been converted into luxury flats. The village club was first a gaol, then a coach house where Lord Leigh's coach was kept while he was at church, before becoming a Reading Room.

Most of the property was let to people who worked at the Abbey and the community was that of a large family with Lord Leigh keeping a fatherly eye over all.

In the 19th century there was a thriving pub called The Stoneleigh Arms in what is now known as Forsythia Cottage, where lads from Coventry would cycle at weekends to enjoy the local brew. Their bicycles would be lined four deep against the bank. One Sunday morning about 1890 when Cordelia, daughter of Lord William Leigh was passing by, the lads called and whistled after her. When Lord William heard this he was so horrified that he ordered the pub to be closed and expressed his wish that there should never be another in the village – which explains the absence of one to this day.

About this time the mill on the Sowe was converted into the village co-operative run by Jo Morris who was not only butcher and baker but also transport operator. He had a covered horse-drawn wagon which left the village at 8.30 am each Friday to take people to Coventry. Three people would sit either side while chickens and occasionally a pig were in the centre. Their destination was The Three Tuns in Hertford Street; it returned promptly at midday.

Many of these traditions began to disappear after the Second World War when two new estates were built and people from outside came to live in Stoneleigh. The largest change to the old way of life took place rapidly after 1979 when Lord Rupert Leigh died and large sums of money had to be found for death duties and to restore the Abbey.

As cottages became vacant they were sold on the open market. Old family names which had existed in the village for generations began to disappear as the young people could not afford these properties. In 1987 the shop closed and now life revolves round the post office, the Village Hall and the Club.

The old order has gone for ever, but new traditions are evolving, such as the annual round of the village each Boxing Day by the Coventry Society of Mummers performing the Stoneleigh Play.

Studley 🦡

The main road through Studley is the Roman Ryknild Street – now the A435. The A435 is also called the Alcester Road and together with Bromsgrove Road and Station Road forms the Studley triangle. Most of the village lay within this triangle, with its green centre, until recent times. Post-war housing estates have spread beyond it, but the green heart is now a school and public playing fields.

Although mentioned in the Domesday Book, only a few ancient buildings survive. One certainly could not call Studley a pretty village but it has a charm all of its own. The river Arrow flows gently by the lovely old church. It has a mill and a castle and a manor house now called Mountbatten House – headquarters of the Royal Life Saving Society.

Studley College, called locally the 'New Castle', was built in 1834 as the home of the Goodricke family, and was until recent

158

years a well known horticultural college for ladies. It is now British Leyland's marketing centre.

Studley is also known for needle-making. Needle Industries' Studley factory is the largest producer of needles in Britain. Traditionally, needles and fishing tackle were made in small factories or 'shops' built behind some of the older houses. In the 1930s most of the small firms were united in Entaco and the small workshops were closed.

One strange thing about Studley – it has 13 pubs! There are also 4 licensed clubs and 2 more pubs in Studley Parish at Mappleborough Green.

Older residents remember Foster's little red vans – 'a shop at your door'. These travelled far and wide to isolated farms and villages taking hard-ware, a hundred and one necessities for the home and garden. They once featured in the National Geographic Magazine.

With great local efforts at fund-raising the swimming pool and Village Hall were built in recent years. The Youth Centre, Health Centre, Library and Fire Station have all increased local facilities, not to mention Entaco Sports & Social Club, built soon after the Second World War.

Tanworth-in-Arden 🌿

Tanworth ('in-Arden' was added in the 19th century for postal convenience) was believed to be Anglo Saxon derived from Tanewotha, the thane's 'worth', or estate. Originally a clearing in the Forest of Arden and hunting ground of the Earls of Warwick, it is now a picturesque village with a friendly atmosphere which attracts many visitors.

The village is set in lovely Warwickshire countryside, still dotted with working farms, some of which have their origins in the 12 moated farm houses which were known in the parish in early medieval times. Still in use is the ancient Codborough Barn and the Danzey windmill which is said to have been in use until the middle of the last century and is now restored and grinding corn at the Avoncroft Museum. Several residents are still employed in farming and allied occupations but the majority now work outside the village at all levels of industry and business.

In the recent past several Tanworth men have earned respect for their expertise, notably Arthur Lewis, internationally renowned breeder of Shire horses; Robert and Alfred Summers, able engineers and millwrights whose skills were sought nationally; and fine carving by Mr Terry is still to be found in many homes.

Today, Tanworth-in-Arden has a garage, a post office with general store, and an off licence, where once there were several thriving shops and small businesses. Several homes retain names which indicate their former use. The Doctor's House, the Old Boot Shop, the Bankhouse which was Burman's Bank in the 18th century, the School House which is still occupied by a teacher from the village school, the Old Work House which was built before 1834 when such provision became compulsory, and the Butts. The heart of the village lies round the triangular green with the war memorial and a young chestnut tree which in time should acquire the stature and character of the one it replaced, which was planted to celebrate Queen Victoria's Jubilee.

First mentioned in the 12th century, the church of St Mary Magdalene still flourishes today, its tower a landmark for miles around. Noted among the vicars are the Rev Phillip Wren, great-grandson of the architect, and Rev Robert Fulwode whose 1341 bequest made provision for 'breade and ale' at an 'annual obit for the Ryngars'. They were clearly as much appreciated then as now for they make a fine sound under Jim Corbett who has been Captain of Ringers for 40 years. The Bell on the Green is the one remaining public house and council houses now stand on the Bell Field which for many years was the home of the Annual Flower Show.

There always has been and still is, great demand for homes in the Whitehead Almshouses. The original four houses were presented to the vicars of Tanworth and Ullenhall in 1873. In addition a complex of a further eight flats was opened in 1987. The Trust now operates its own Housing Association but the conditions of residency remain almost identical to those laid down originally. A thriving Church Primary School is still partially maintained by the Tanworth Educational Foundation, which has

Umberslade Hall, Tanworth-in-Arden

its roots in charitable donations of land and money made over several centuries. Chairman of the Foundation is F. D. Muntz who is Lord of the Manor of Tanworth and also holds the living of the parish church.

Close to the centre of the village lies Umberslade, home of the Archer family for at least six centuries. At the end of the 17th century Andrew Archer rebuilt the Hall which is now converted into luxury flats. In the grounds is an obelisk built in 1749 by Thomas Archer, probably to commemorate his elevation to the peerage. It is from the Archer family that Tanworth claims its most famous resident, Sir Simon Archer, a renowned antiquarian who initiated work on *The Antiquites of Warwickshire* ultimately compiled by Sir William Dugdale.

Temple Grafton ✥

Piping Pebworth
Dancing Marston
Haunted Hillborough
Hungry Grafton
Dodging Exhall
Papist Wixford
Beggarly Broom
Drunken Bidford

Temple Grafton is situated 5 miles to the north-west of Stratford-upon-Avon (off the A422). It is still a peaceful, unspoilt village, despite the recent increase in through traffic due to the Stratford northern by-pass opened in 1987. The village's name is said to derive from the Knights Templars and Knights Hospitallers who once owned the church. Why the village was called 'hungry' is not known but it has been suggested that in Shakespearean times, when the verse above is said to have been written, the land was not very fertile and provided only a poor living for the farming community.

Temple Grafton is one of the villages with a claim to be considered as the place where William Shakespeare was married, but there is no conclusive evidence for this.

Major changes took place in the village between 1855 and 1875. A new Baptist chapel was built. In 1874 Temple Grafton Court was built on the site of the former Manor House by J. W. Carlile who also rebuilt St Andrew's church and provided the village with a new school. Several cottages and a vicarage were also built during these years. There were no further big changes until, between the wars, houses in Croft Lane were built.

Today farming continues to be an important activity but in the years since the Second World War there have been many changes in farming methods, the type of crops produced and in the use of farm buildings and land – all of which have had a profound effect on the appearance of the village and on the life of the community. Farm buildings have been converted into dwellings, one farm now offers bed and breakfast, arable land has given way to large fields, and many hedgerows and wooded areas have disappeared. With mechanisation less labour is needed on the farms and traditional jobs and trades associated with farming have almost disappeared. Most villagers now commute to the local towns.

Temple Grafton and its close neighbour, Ardens Grafton, were once largely self-supporting with a bakery, a grocer, a cider press, a malt house and a blacksmith. People are now totally dependent on shops in the local towns. The post office/general store finally closed down in 1987.

The village of Temple Grafton

The village school continues to play a vital role in community life and draws children from several neighbouring villages.

The cricket club, founded over a hundred years ago, is still flourishing and continues to play on the original cricket ground at Grafton Court.

However great the social and economic changes, the scenic beauty of the area remains. Temple Grafton and Ardens Grafton lie along a ridge of hills and command superb views of the countryside to the west with the Malvern hills just visible in the distance, and to the south-east, over the Avon valley towards the Cotswolds.

Tredington

Tredington is a village with a population of approximately 502 situated on the A34 between Stratford-upon-Avon and Shipston-on-Stour, with the Roman Fosse Way lying to the west.

The earliest reference to Tredington in AD 757 calls it Tredinc-gtun. By AD 964 the name had become Tyrdintun. The name is believed to have originated from the farmstead or village of Tyrdda.

The dominating feature is the church with its golden spire being a landmark for miles around. It was built in 961 and dedicated to St Gregory. There are traces of Norman and Saxon stonework and also the remains of bullets in the vast oak door, reputed to have been left by the Roundheads during their fight with the Royalists.

At the time when the two starch factories and the mill employed many of the villagers, there was a butcher's shop, a bakery, a wheelwright and a blacksmith, but now there is only one friendly general store with a post office.

There is a story related by the grandparent of a local resident that, at the turn of the century, there lived an old lady in a cottage on the main road, who had witch's powers. On one occasion the coalman refused to leave a bag of coal because previous supplies had not been paid for. She pleaded: 'Jus' leave me one bag to last I thro' the week'. When he still refused she said 'If yo' don't leave me a bag, yo' 'osses won't budge when yo' reaches 'em!' Well he found no amount of pulling, pushing, coaxing or swearing moved them an inch, so he went back and said 'Yo' can 'ave all they bags ont' cart if you'll only mek them 'osses move'. 'No' she said, 'Jus' one bag to last me the week is all I want'. And sure enough, after he'd delivered the bag, they 'osses moved off without any trouble!

The old school (complete with bell) is now a private house and the Council built a new school on the west side in the 1960s, but this still has strong connections with the church.

The rector has to serve 5 villages, with three church buildings: Armscote, Blackwell, Darlingscote and Newbold-on-Stour, with about 2 miles journey between each village. The two busy main roads hinder accessibility.

Blackwell has a population of about 60, with a brick-built village hall and a Methodist chapel. Armscote is a hamlet with approximately 40 residents, has one pub and a Friends' Meeting House which holds a meeting once a year. Darlingscote, with a population of less than 60, has a Chapel of Ease, with a pretty churchyard with cowslips, primroses, daisies and buttercups heralding the spring. It has a club and a cricket club, but the residents now are mostly farmers or weekend cottagers.

Tysoe 🌿

Tysoe is divided into three parts. Approaching from the foot of Sunrising Hill on the A422 Banbury/Stratford road, one comes to Lower Tysoe (known in days gone by as Temple Tysoe, reflecting the fact that lands were held by the Knights Templars of Balsall). Carrying straight on the traveller reaches Middle (or Church) Tysoe, where are clustered the church, inn, village hall, shops, Fire Station and a fine Methodist church and hall built in 1970. Finally there is Upper (or Over) Tysoe, astride the Shipston/Brailes road. From here one has a view of Tysoe's one remaining windmill, and beyond the windmill lies Compton Wynyates, a great Tudor mansion and now the seat of the Marquis of Northampton.

The house, of mellow brick, is prettily sited against wooded hills. The use of brick in 'stone country' is probably due to King Henry VIII's having given the ruined castle of Fulbroke (near Warwick) to Sir William Compton, who in turn salvaged materials and used them at Compton. Unfortunately, this beautiful house is no longer open to the public.

The unusual name of Tysoe actually means 'spur of land dedicated to Tiw', a Germanic god of war, from whom Tuesday takes its name. Around the year AD 600 the conquering Saxons are believed to have cut a huge war horse into the red soil of the hillside, resulting in the area becoming known as the Vale of the Red Horse. The horse-figure seems to have been 'opposite to the East window of Tysoe Church', towards Sunrising Hill. Palm Sunday was the traditional day for annual scouring, but around 1800 the site was ploughed and is now lost for ever under woodland.

William the Conqueror gave Tysoe to one of his followers, Robert de Stafford, and in size and importance it ranked (along with Brailes) next to Warwick. It is a village where the appearance of the fields, with marked 'ridge and furrow' effect, provides clear evidence of the medieval system of open field cultivation. These field patterns are particularly noticeable when the sun is low, or after a light covering of snow.

The church dates from the 11th century, or even earlier, and is dedicated to the Assumption of the Blessed Virgin. There is a Norman doorway, a 14th century octagonal font, a churchyard cross (probably 15th century) and an 18th century bellcote to house a Sanctus bell. The building and contents are lovingly cared for.

The village school takes approximately 150 children from a wide area, covering eight communities.

The lane leading from the churchyard to Peacock Inn is known as Saddledon Street. Local legend describes how, on the eve of the Battle of Edgehill in 1642, a squadron of Royalist cavalry rode through Tysoe, helped themselves to fresh-baked bread, unsaddled their horses in a farmyard and enjoyed a meal of bread, beer and cider! Thoroughly refreshed, they resaddled their horses and went to join King Charles. The lane was thereafter called Saddling Street, and eventually Saddledon Street! A good story anyway.

Next to the post office, in Main Street, is the small Reading Room, bought as a memorial to the men of Tysoe who served in the First World War, and here are their names, proudly recorded in stone. The Second World War Memorial is close by, in front of the police sation.

To the right of the War Memorial can be seen a niche which housed a tap for the first piped water supply, and, typical of its period, it bears texts, one being, 'My soul is athirst for God, yea even for the living God', Ps.42.2. Another niche, opposite to the church and at the entrance to the former vicarage, has a seat on either side, presumably for the use of the more elderly or infirm as they waited their turn at the tap, and here there is the text 'Rest in the Lord and wait patiently', Ps.37.7. Did someone have his tongue in cheek?

As a result of the enclosure of the open fields a charitable trust was formed, known as the 'Town Lands', and monies are still distributed.

In the 1880s an Allotments Association was formed, and after much perseverance and many promises of land being found for the project, the Association was eventually able to rent land. This was a tremendous boon to the agricultural workers and others, in very hard times, and the land is still known by the name it was unofficially given during the struggles: 'The Promised Land'.

Ufton 🌿

Ufton is a small village and includes Bascote Heath in its parish. It is situated on the main Northampton to Warwick road, 2½ miles west of Southam, with a population of approximately 220. The name Ufton has undergone many changes. It is thought the name is of Saxon origin, being recorded as Ulchtune in the Domesday Book.

The church as it now stands was built in the 14th century but a Saxon church stood on the present site as far back as 1042.

There have been two charities in Ufton, the first in 1768 when the benefactor was unknown and the second being Thomas Horley, who set up his charity in 1877 to provide coal and warm clothing for the poor of the parish.

The school was closed in the early 1970s and an amenities committee was set up to help to keep the community together. The first project was in 1975 when the bus shelter was built by local craftsmen in stone in an attempt to thwart vandalism – it was a great success.

At one time the village was owned by the Spencer family of Althorpe Hall (the Princess of Wales' family).

One of the highlights in the village was a Flower Show, formed in 1912 when eight large marquees were hired at a cost of £5 each and as many as 3,000 people paid to attend.

A phantom coach and horses is said to ride through the village and down the hill at certain times but it hasn't been seen lately!

Ullenhall 🦚

The village of Ullenhall, it is believed, was originally built around the 13th century church of St Mark. At the time of the plague the village moved to its present site, the church of St Mark now known as 'The Old Chapel' being reduced to its present size in 1875.

In 1964 the Hobditch Causeway (a Roman Road) was found to run through the garden of Wild Pear Cottage at Dean's Green.

Barrells Hall was built in 1580 and enlarged in 1770. Its most famous resident was Lady Luxborough who was banished there in 1736 by her husband Robert Knight, famous for his family connections with the South Sea Bubble financial disaster. Since her death Lady Luxborough is reputed to haunt the ruins. Barrells Hall was badly burnt in 1933.

Hall End Farm dates from the 17th century. In 1808 John Booth was murdered there by his brother William, who was sentenced to death. The hangman failed in his task twice, before succeeding on the third occasion. During the Second World War Mrs Roosevelt (wife of the President of the USA) secretly visited the Land Girls stationed at Oldberrow Farm.

The Newton family built St Mary's church and the vicarage in 1875 and the Church of England School and adjacent school house in 1876. The vicarage and land were sold for development in 1973. The school was closed in 1987 despite a vigorous campaign to save it.

There are various charities connected with Ullenhall that are still administered. St Mark's Charity, whose income is from cot-

168

Gentleman's Lane House at Ullenhall

tage and land rents, is divided between the Parochial Church Council and the Parish Council. Francis Brittain Charity is to buy one gown and one petticoat each for six poor women of the Parish – all from £3 a year. The Agar and Herring Aid in Sickness Charity has its proceeds divided between neighbouring parishes.

The Village Hall was built in 1935 on land given by Mr and Mrs Barber. The Hall remains to this day the property of the village and is the centre for village activities.

Over the years the village has had its own post office cum general stores and two other village shops, one combined with an off-licence but these all closed in the early 1980s. There has also been a bakery, a blacksmith, a fish and chip shop, a haberdashery, a cafe, a riding school, a boat builder and a garage. All are now past history and the tiny cottages that once housed these businesses have been converted into sought-after modernised cottages.

The Winged Spur remains a valuable focal point, the licencee and his wife taking an active part in the village. The fortunes of their two race horses, *Mr Boot* and *Spur*, are followed with keen interest by the community.

The population of Ullenhall has reduced over the last 50 years and is just under 400. Housing varies, only 2 cottages remain as they were built (date unknown) and there are two small council developments, now partly owner occupied, modern houses and bungalows and several character houses and cottages.

One proud boast of Ullenhall is Crowley's Oak – reputed to have been planted over 1,000 years ago.

Walton ﹏

The tiny village of Walton is a rarity, an excellent example of an estate village, with its buildings still complete, each turning its best face towards the great house, Walton Hall, and its working face to the road. There you can find 15 cottages, plus the old estate office, forge, school house, farm, and the laundry (now renamed Lawnderry House!). The Home Farm, and the Keeper's Cottage are there, together with the Old Rectory, where the present owner, Sir Richard Hamilton, has lived since 1962. His wife, Lady Elizabeth Hamilton has written fascinating books and articles on the history of the Mordaunt family, and the Hall.

There has been some kind of settlement at Walton, on the little river Dene, between the Fosse Way and Wellesbourne, since Iron Age times. The field to the south of the House, the site of the deserted village of Walton d'Eivile, is still known as Old Town.

Walton Hall has not always looked as it does today. It was given a new face in 1862 by the well known Victorian architect and restorer, Gilbert Scott, whose design in the Gothic Revival 'Middle Pointed' style is very reminiscent of 13th and 14th century work. The lake was excavated 13 years later, and in the grounds are a distinctive bridge, known as Gog Bridge, a bath house, and an ice house, as well as the pretty little church of St James, built during the mid-18th century on the site of a previous church.

During this century the Hall has seen many changes. A family home for the widowed Lady Mordaunt for 50 years, it was used by the army during the Second World War (with Lady Mordaunt and her daughter retaining part of it) and was for a time the headquarters of the Free Czechoslovakian Army. Later it was used by the Territorial Army, but when the War Department lease ran out in 1962, it was let to St Vincent's Girls School, and later made into a hotel. Now it is converted to timeshare apartments and brings people from many places to enjoy its rural setting.

One person who knew many happenings in the close knit community was Marjorie Newbery. Her husband Tom was a groom, and in 1926 she started a shop in the front room of their cottage. Here the post box was installed, and daily necessities could be purchased. She retired and closed the shop in 1979, and now the nearest shop is in Wellesbourne. The village school was built in 1831, and by 1860 had 50 children on its roll. Now the few school age children in Walton go daily to Kineton. Post, milk and refuse disposal services come in from outside.

Today the houses are still owned by the estate, but the people who live in them seldom work at Walton Hall. The influence of the Hall is still there. It brings people through the village, cars disturb the utter peace of the valley, but Walton remains wonderfully quiet.

Walton 🌿

A mystery surrounds the very name of the village of Warton! No mention of Warton is found in the Domesday Book (1086), though the nearby village of Orton-on-the-Hill is chronicled under the name of Wartone, leading many students of local history to believe that Warton, as it is at present, did not exist at that time, a view that is borne out by the fact that only one medieval building, with a very small part of another, exists in Warton to this day.

It is probable that the present Warton was part of the estate of the owner of the land at Orton, and that the windmill for grinding corn which may well have existed at Warton at that time (there was a windmill here until recent times) was also within the demesne of the then Lord of the Manor of 'Wartone'. It may also be significant that the oldest public house, The Fox and Dogs, is at Little Warton (once a hamlet in its own right, though now an integral part of Warton Village). The other two, The Boot Inn, and The Hatter's Arms are of relatively recent origin.

The agricultural land surrounding the present village has always been noted for its great productivity, owing much to the fact that in the Middle Ages it was entirely under water for most of the winter and spring. The annual floods bring with them a highly fertile silt-marl, in which farmers, allotment-holders, and gardeners come across the typical rounded pebbles of a river valley. It is possible that only the advent of coalmining in the early years of the 19th century led to the land being readily available for cultivation, as it may have been the many shallow mines that caused the unforeseen drainage of the area!

As in many villages all over England there is the ubiquitous apochryphal legend of the 'pig on the wall, watching the band go by', which may in Warton's case have an element of truth – pigs are still bred and reared here.

The present Holy Trinity (Church of England) church at Warton dates only from the middle of the 19th century and there is no evidence of a previous church on the site, or even in the village, though at one time there were no less than three non-conformist chapels. These were probably erected as a result of Warton's becoming a village inhabited by miners, though there was no mine in Warton itself.

That there was little if any proper sanitation in the miners' two-up-and-two-down cottages is borne out by evidence that soon after the church was built, a significantly large number of whole families were buried within the space of a few years. This was during the cholera epidemic of 1850–60. A row of gravestones bearing the same surname, Hull, and the ages ranging from a few months to 45 years or so, is a sad reminder of those times.

Most of the inhabitants work in nearby towns and cities, principally Birmingham, Tamworth and Leicester. Though at one time it was possible to purchase virtually all one's household requirements in the village – there was a butcher, a baker, a shoemaker, a blacksmith, a garage and petrol station, a tailor, a general store – these have disappeared one by one, leaving only a greengrocer and the general store which is also the post office. This, too, is reputed to be again under threat of closure, though it serves a very large area – without it Warton would be even less of a 'real village' than it is now.

The earliest school in the village was opened in 1832, and was held in the schoolmaster's house, which still exists, though it is now a private dwelling-house. Behind it is the village school, built about the time of the Education Act of 1870, and replaced in 1975 by a new First School.

Water Orton 🍂

The village of Water Orton has grown steadily through the years, its early name being 'Overton', meaning 'a settlement upon the river bank'. This area of high land lies either side of Old Church Road on the south side of the river Tame.

Two half-timbered buildings, known as The Chestnuts, circa 15th century, and Wakefield House, circa 16th century, can still be seen on the southern edge of the old village. To the north of these properties is the now abandoned graveyard. Once within its walls stood the first church buildings. Early records show that a Chapel of Ease was here in 1347. This attractive title meant that the chapel as a more convenient place for the villagers to worship in, rather than travelling all the way to Aston, where the 'mother' church could be found. For many years, Water Orton belonged to the huge parish of Aston, then in August 1871 it was formed into an ecclesiastical parish.

The base and shaft of an ancient stone cross can still be seen in the old graveyard. This edifice has survived the chapel and was once the open air pulpit used by the travelling preachers of long ago to spread the gospel to the settlers.

Many pottery shards dug up from the garden of Wakefield House some years ago were dated as early as the 13th century. Some are possibly of Roman origin, making Overton a place with a very long history. The word 'Water' first appears in documents of the 16th century and today, after the slightest shower, it can be seen why it was added!

Almost a quarter of a mile to the south lies the village green, another interesting area. At its eastern corner once stood an old cottage, demolished in 1951. Records dated it back to the 13th century and, with solid (brick) upper floors, it may have been a malt house, which would have been used for storing barley grain ready for the making of ale. Another feature of the cottage was a huge baking oven and deep garden well. The village school overlooks the green from the south and was built during 1878. Several modern extensions have made it into a large educational centre.

The village has two public houses, The Digby Hotel built about 1860 and The Dog (1722). Two others, both of which could be found in the Coleshill Road, have long since disappeared, their sites now occupied by new buildings.

It was, of course, the railway that assured the village of a future. Until 1842 this was just a scattering of little cottages and farms. Water Orton station brought in visitors and new residents by the score. In no time at all a small farming settlement had become a busy little village. Many large gentlemen's residences were built; all, alas, no longer standing; their sites now containing flats, a clinic, houses, a Methodist chapel, maisonettes and a road. A large and very busy railway siding to the west of the village offered many jobs to Water Orton during the steam era. It was always said that if you worked on the railway you were well off!

Today employment can be found on the huge industrial estate only a mile away near Coleshill, or a few hundred yards over the old 'Vesey' river bridge at the growing factory by the river Tame. This large complex produces many goods made of UPVC, including the fast expanding trade of window frames.

The railway station sees much activity as does the 109 year old church, sadly now without its spire. The Methodist chapel (1868) is well attended and there is also the Catholic church hall of St John the Baptist (1966).

When the M6 relief road is built Water Orton will be completely surrounded by motorways, securing its future as a village forever!

Weethley

Weethley comes from an Anglo-Saxon word meaning withy clearing or withywood, and is mentioned in the Domesday Book of 1086. It is situated approximately 3 miles from Alcester along the Ridgeway, between Redditch and Evesham. It has always been a small place, although from the contours of the land it is presumed there were more dwellings in the vicinity at one time. Some of the cottages are 17th century timber framed, although most of them have now been renovated and brought in line with today's building regulations, while still retaining their old world charm. At one time all the land belonged to The Marquis of Hertford who owns Ragley Hall.

The church of St James was rebuilt in late 13th century style in 1857, and is located on a hillside, which is the highest point in the area and has beautiful views of the Cotswolds from the porch. Just outside the gate is a pond with lilies and a thriving family of ducks. This tiny church holds a congregation of approximately 100. A service is held at the church every Sunday and, according to records, has been held without interruption since before 1900. Unfortunately, this record was broken in 1967 by the outbreak of Foot and Mouth Disease which threatened the churchwarden's stock. Although his farm was spared the church was inaccessible for six weeks.

Each year on the 1st May more than 20 Morris dancers and musicians and about 60 onlookers gather on the hillside by the church to revive a centuries-old ceremony to greet the dawn of the first day of May. The White Hart Morris Men, who are based at Redditch, revived the ancient tradition in 1980. They dance for almost an hour, gather in the church for coffee and then adjourn to The Cross Keys public house in Alcester.

Although Weethley is only a very small place it has a lot to offer: peace, tranquillity, the beauty of the changing seasons and, of course, the wildlife – the birds, the rabbits and the deer. There have been very few changes during the last century and it is to be hoped that during the next century Weethley will remain much the same.

Welford-on-Avon
& Weston-on-Avon

Along the river Avon, appriximately 5 miles westward from Stratford, are the villages of Weston and Welford-on-Avon. These two villages consist of timbered, thatched, black and white cottages, typical of Shakespeare country, with Victorian and modern properties scattered in between.

Welford was originally established in Saxon times by monks from Deerhurst in Gloucestershire and is the larger village of the two. Weston is a small cluster of houses and a church, nearby. Over the centuries most of the villagers were small holders, self sufficient, and not beholden to a Lord of the Manor. Local trades recorded were farmworkers, shoemakers, spinners, cider makers, needle polishers, glove makers and blacksmiths.

The original Saxon church in Welford was built by the Priory of Deerhurst. The church, as seen today, is perpendicular style, on Norman foundations. In the church is a Saxon font bowl, and a carved wooden screen dedicated to the 'Fallen of the First World War'.

Weston church was built in the 15th century in Perpendicular style by John Greville of nearby Milcote Manor. Joseph Green, vicar of Weston in 1735 was an influential public figure in Stratford and discovered and copied William Shakespeare's will – a copy of which is in the British Museum.

On the village green in Welford is a maypole, 65 feet tall – one of only five in the country. It is known to have existed in the 14th century. The original wooden maypole was struck by lightning and blown down, and was replaced with a metal one with a running fox weathervane. It is painted, red white and blue stripe, every 10 years. Village schoolchildren dance around the maypole annually in July.

Over the centuries tales have emerged of characters living in Welford & Weston. There is the 'Wicked Loddy' – the bogey man the children lived in fear of. The son of Sir Edward Greville of Milcote Manor, he was the notorious Lodvic Greville who was pressed to death with stones in 1589 for murder.

Welford & Weston is a busy thriving community today. Welford has a population of approximately 1,500. It has a post office, village stores, butcher, school, church and three pubs, and has won the Warwickshire Best Kept Village competition.

Tourism is the main industry providing employment in Stratford and the Cotswolds for the locals and new cottage industries have evolved in the village itself.

Wellesbourne ✒

Wellesbourne lies within 10 miles of Stratford, Warwick, Leamington and Kineton – a large village which, although not notably pretty, has attractive quiet corners and a charm that increases upon closer inspection. It seems initially a village without a centre and maps often show two names, Wellesbourne Mountford and Wellesbourne Hastings. The two Wellesbournes take their names from local families, no longer remembered as often as they were, for the village is now known to all but cartographers simply as Wellesbourne.

Lying to the north, Wellesbourne Hastings had at its heart the church of St Peter, with its 15th century tower, set in a pleasant little side road between the Old Vicarage, the Malt House, and The King's Head. This hostelry, despite modern additions on the northern aspect, still gives a rural feeling to the end of Church Street, where some of the older houses stand, and where there was once a charter for an annual fair.

Wellesbourne Mountford was the southern part of the modern village, centred around the picturesque Chestnut Square, with a distinctive thatched pub, The Stag's Head, in one corner. It was in Chestnut Square that Joseph Arch, in 1872, inaugurated the first trade union for agricultural workers, an event which is still commemorated with an annual parade, and marked by an unusual memorial – a plaque in the bus shelter. The buildings in Church Walk and Chapel Street are very much as he would have known them.

Further south than Chestnut Square is the sports field, with regular matches of bowls, football and hockey, as well as cricket on a green which boasts of being among the oldest in Britain, and was mentioned in *Tom Brown's Schooldays*.

During the Second World War farmland to the south-west of the main village was requisitioned as an airfield and used by the RAF and the Canadian airforce. Following this, the airfield was used for occasional flying and then developed as a small aerodrome for light aircraft. The old Dovehouse Farm, the domestic site, was not suitable for return to its former use and was finally used for housing in the 1980s. Local names, and those of the aircraft that flew from the aerodrome, have been preserved in the street names.

The two halves merge at the river Dene, a shallow river, once prone to high floods, which meets the Avon in Charlecote. It is crossed by a two lane bridge, which marks both the centre of the village and the link between its two wards. The separate Parish Councils were amalgamated in 1947, and the amalgamated Council also covers Walton, an old estate village lying in seclusion 1½ miles to the south-east.

Just by the bridge is Dog Close, its name connecting it with The Talbot, just across the road. It was here the landlord originally grew the ingredients for the beer. Mostly now it is used for grazing, but the occasional village carnival takes place where once the ground was levelled to accommodate the tug of war teams. Today's residents regard the field as the 'green lung' of Wellesbourne and preserve the open space as part of a conservation area.

Although not strictly within the boundaries of the village, Wellesbourne is known internationally because of the National Vegetable Research Station, now part of the Institute of Horticultural Research, which uses much of the open farmland to the west of the village. Here scientists work on problems connected with the breeding and raising of vegetables, and have given many new varieties to the grower, as well as preserving historic ones in a special gene bank.

Recent additions to Wellesbourne, starting with several developments in the 1960s and followed in the 1980s by the 800 houses on the Dovehouse estate, meant that by 1988 the population was well over 5,000. Despite this, Wellesbourne is still proud to call itself a village, and retains the feel of a village.

Whatcote

Whatcote is small and peaceful, lying between Oxhill and Idlicote, but small or not, it is recorded in Domesday Book.

The Royal Oak is 17th century and a very popular venue. Farms, houses and bungalows cluster round the ancient parish church of St Peter and the little Methodist church built in 1905.

It is interesting to look at St Peter's, surrounded by fields, (on a site which has seen a church for nearly 1,000 years) and to realise that the present building yet managed to get itself hit by a stray enemy bomb at the time of the Coventry blitz in late 1940! An old font, which is Norman or even earlier, was damaged by the German bomb, but has been skilfully repaired.

Marks on the east wall of the tower exterior show clearly how the pitch of the roof has been altered at some time, and one can also see, carved into the tower battlements, an inverted chevron on a shield – the coat-of-arms of the Earls of Stafford. The Staffords were Lords of the Manor until about 1520 when the village was sold to the Northamptons. The shaft of the old preaching cross is medieval, but is now mounted on an octagonal base, probably 18th century.

Willoughby

Willoughby is a village on the very edge of Warwickshire. The border with Northamptonshire is only a few yards along the A45 on the way to Daventry. Consequently, it may not be known to many people outside its own area. However, one way of introducing the village is by a question. What have Willoughby and Lilliput in common? The answer is not just that both are small places but something much more interesting. The answer is Dean Swift, Jonathan Swift of *Gulliver's Travels*.

The story is told in Willoughby that Dean Swift used to travel from London to Holyhead by road, en route for Ireland. He would sometimes spend a night at The Three Crosses Inn at Willoughby in order to break his journey. Jonathan Swift was an arrogant and irascible character but he apparently met his match in the landlady of The Three Crosses. On one occasion she so angered him that he wrote with his diamond ring on the window pane for the attention of the landlord

You have three crosses
On your door
Hang up your wife
And she'll make four.

Thereafter the inn became known as the Four Crosses and there are four crosses on the wall of the present building which is now a transport dormitory.

Willoughby is a pleasant place to live. It is far enough from any large town for it to preserve a sense of rural peace. But large centres like Coventry, Northampton and Leamington Spa are all easily accessible in this age of the motor car. Most people work outside the village although a number operate small businesses from their homes.

Cricket has been played in Willoughby for over a hundred years but the present club was founded in 1901. This club has a good local reputation for excellence of cricket and club spirit and it attracts players, social members and spectators from quite a wide area.

This is an ancient village, being mentioned in Domesday Book and the records of Magdalen College which go back to the 15th century. Vale House and The Rose Inn are probably the oldest dwellings. The inn is at least 400 years old.

The church is very ancient indeed. There is a record of its existence in 1215 although, of course, parts of the building were added at different times. The lychgate, which looks old, was built in 1977 to commemorate the Queen's Silver Jubilee. It is built of weathered stone to harmonise with the church. A very interesting feature of the church is the carillon or turret clock. This was brought from Southam in 1724. It was out of use for nearly 50 years but was restored to working order in 1983. Most of the cost was subscribed by the Willoughby Foundation, which forms part of the ancient and munificent Willoughby Charities. Five well known tunes can be played upon the carillon.

The Willoughby Charities were established by John Hayward and his wife Margaret in 1437. John Brook, another benefactor is recorded as having made his charitable bequest in 1535, during the reign of Henry VIII. John is remembered in the name of Brooks Close which was a field adjoining the churchyard. It is now an attractive curve of bungalows built in the 1960s but still carrying the name of Brooks Close.

The name Willoughby was probably better known when the main LNER line passed through Braunston and Willoughby Station. Line and station are no longer to be seen so we are left with just the name Willoughby, said to be derived from Willowbec because of the willow trees that still grow beside the little brook which flows along by the village street.

Wilmcote 🌿

Wilmcote is a village 3 miles north of Stratford-upon-Avon with a population of about 1,000.

In the 19th century 55 per cent of the population worked at the local quarries producing high quality floor stone and marble known as blue lias, some of which was used at the Palace of Westminster in London.

There were five public houses serving a small community. Now there are just two, The Masons Arms and The Swan House Hotel.

The gem in the heart of Wilmcote is of course Mary Arden's House, the childhood home of Shakespeare's mother. It is a beautiful half-timbered house of the 16th century. It was once a hall house and would have looked rather different in those days. Bedrooms have been added at a later date, the thatched roof replaced by handmade tiles and a stone floor laid. Originally, the house would have had a solar, a room for sleeping, over the kitchen for the use of the family. Servants and workers would have slept on the floor around the fire in the centre of the room, the smoke finding its way out through a hole in the thatch. It would have had an earth floor with rushes scattered upon it.

As the winter wore on more rushes were added, building up into a sort of compost heap, full of vermin. When springtime came around (and the floor was high in more senses than one!), it was time for spring cleaning. The rotting rushes would be thrown onto the midden outside the back door. The interior of the house would be white-washed, including the beams. It is a fairly modern idea to leave the beams unwhitewashed.

Today the house is open to the public and furnished with some lovely old oak pieces. There is an old board table, a hutch cupboard and a monk's bench made about 1480. It is a farmhouse and the farm buildings are full of things of interest, artifacts and farm implements collected over many years.

One of the best of the buildings is the dovecote. As Robert Arden was the lord of the manor he was the only man in the village with a dovecote. It has over 600 pigeon holes and at nesting time would house about 3,000 birds. (With a bit of luck his pigeons would have fed on his neighbours' land, come home to roost in his dovecote and ended up on his table!)

Mary was the youngest of Robert Arden's eight daughters. Having no sons when he died, his only unmarried daughter living at home, Mary, inherited her father's property.

St Andrew's Church, Wilmcote

John Shakespeare, hearing of this heiress at Wilmcote came hotfoot from Stratford to court her. They were married and he carried her off to Stratford where he was in business as a glover and leather worker. William was their eldest son.

The house remained in the family, being occupied for a while by Mary's sister who was married to a man called Edkins. There are still people called Edkins living in the area.

Most of the estate has long since broken up but the house, buildings and the Glebe farmhouse next door are now owned by the Shakespeare Birthplace Trust and open throughout the year as a museum attracting visitors from all over the world.

Wilmcote is one of the few small villages to retain its railway station and still has a regular service from Stratford.

Alongside the railway runs the Stratford Canal, built in the early 1800s to carry the limestone from the quarry and up to 500,000 tons of coal a year from the Midland coal fields. Until recently the stretch of canal from Stratford to Wilmcote was in the care of the National Trust but has been taken over by British Waterways. After years of neglect it is now carrying many holiday boats on their way to Stratford to join the river.

Wishaw 🌿

Wishaw is almost part of Sutton Coldfield, and was mentioned in the Domesday Survey of 1086 when it was known as Witscaga, meaning 'mountain ash by the curving hollow'. The present population is under 200, less than that recorded in the Domesday Survey.

From Edward the Confessor's time Wishaw and nearby Moxhull had been manors of the Knights Templars, and in 1257 Wishaw was granted to Walter de Beresford, whose descendants were still living in the parish in the 20th century. They are commemorated in Wishaw church, dedicated to St Chad, Bishop of Lichfield from 669 to 672. Built on the site of an old Roman church, originally it would have been constructed of timber, but the earliest part of the present building dates back to the 13th century with later additions from the 15th to 19th centuries. One interesting feature of the church is a hagioscope, or 'lepers' squint'. From here, lepers would be able to see the altar from outside the church and watch the preparation and administration of the sacrament. The church bells would also ring the curfew for the charcoal burners of the Forest of Arden, of which this area was once part.

The church also has a memorial to Thomas Baylis, the village schoolmaster for 31 years, who 'amassed a plentiful fortune' and in 1744 donated several gifts of money to the church and the poor of the parish and '10 shillings a year for one scholar's expenses at the school'. The school, now Church Farm, was a few yards from the church.

The old Cock Inn, a well-known local landmark, has been enlarged and modernised in recent years and was reputedly one of Dick Turpin's hiding places. There were two other coaching inns in the village, both on the former London Road (now the main A446): The Mother Redcap Inn and The Green Man. Both are still standing but have been private houses for many years.

The Memorial Hall was built by public subscription in 1923 to honour the fallen of the First World War. Almost next door are the former workhouses, now two pretty cottages.

One of the oldest buildings in Wishaw, and indeed in the whole of Sutton Coldfield, is The Grove, which has unusual cruck trusses (a type of oak beam) naturally curved to form an arch which support the walls and roof. Other interesting buildings in the village are located in Wiggins Hill Road: the Old Barn, a black-and-white half-timbered cottage and barn; Wiggins Hill Farm which has an unusual curved Dutch gable; and Quaker Cottage, formerly a Quaker Meeting House built in 1724 which served the many Quakers living in the area at that time. Now a private house, a Quaker burial ground is reputedly situated near the garden wall.

The well-known Belfry Hotel, Golf and Leisure Centre is on the site of Old Moxhull Hall. This was once the home of one of the district's most prominent families, the Rylands, but was destroyed by the family earlier this century as there was a superstition that it was responsible for the deaths of several family members. New Moxhull Hall was built nearby, and is now also a hotel.

The Belfry is now the home of the Professional Golfers' Association and its Brabazon Course was made famous in 1985 when the European team beat the USA in the Ryder Cup.

Nowadays, Wishaw has no school, village shop, or even a bus service, but it is still a thriving community. The majority of the village lies within the Green Belt and is still largely agricultural. Unlike its near neighbours Middleton, Curdworth and Minworth, Wishaw has not seen any new housing development in recent years, but it sadly lives under the threat of the encroaching Midlands motorway network.

Wolvey ✺

The village of Wolvey lies almost on the boundary between Warwickshire and Leicestershire. To the north-east of the village runs Watling Street, now the A5, and just across the parish boundary to the south is the Fosse Way. Because of this unique crossing point between two major ancient highways Wolvey has always been a village of transit, a stopping place for travellers rather than a centre of more stable activities. This pattern must have developed centuries ago. Abbey Farm, just to the north of Wolvey has a neolithic barrow on its lands and the largest scatter of flints anywhere in Warwickshire.

The proximity of the two great roads meant that great armies must have passed close by or even through the village. In 1470 Edward IV fought a battle on Wolvey Heath, was defeated and captured by Warwick the Kingmaker and taken on to imprisonment in Middleham Castle, in Yorkshire, home of the legendary Richard III. But extant records also include happier occasions, such as the welcoming of Queen Elizabeth I 'with a great company of nobles' in the centre of the village by the Mayor of the City of Coventry and his colleagues 'in skarlett gownes with foot clothes' in 1566, as she progressed from Leicester and crossed the county boundary.

Like so many Warwickshire villages, Wolvey today is a mixture of architectural styles from different periods and its small population includes descendants of earlier inhabitants besides many newcomers attracted by the bracing winds that once made Wolvey famous for its proliferation of windmills (now, alas, all vanished), its lush farmland and its pedigree. For Wolvey, as the name indicates, was once a Saxon settlement and the name may mean 'enclosure to protect flocks from wolves', proving that when the Forest of Arden stretched across the county, Wolvey offered a haven, a place of respite in the wildness. The first mention of Wolvey (Ulvetha) in the Domesday Book of 1086 notes that there were 15 villagers and one priest.

The most mysterious and most poignant story from Wolvey's past is the strange case of Lady Dorothy Smythe who, as Dugdale claims in his *Antiquities of Warwickshire*, published in 1656 'was burnt at a Stake near the Hermitage on Wolvey heath (towards the side of Shirford lordship) where the country people to this day shew the place'. Dugdale's 'Shirford' was, in fact, Shelford, a manor just outside the boundary of Wolvey and of which nothing remains today except the name, which belongs to one of the local farms. Lady Dorothy, married to Sir Walter Smythe, had been mistress of Shelford until her death in 1555. Her brutal death was in consequence of being found guilty of her husband's murder two years earlier.

Wootton Wawen

Despite its postal address, which would have the unwary believe it is part of the suburban sprawl of the West Midlands, Wootton Wawen has its roots secure in the soil of Warwickshire. To this day the village owes its allegiance to that county – whatever the post office might say.

Wootton Wawen has strong claims to being one of the oldest villages in Warwickshire. The village takes its name from the Saxon words 'wudu', meaning wood, and 'tun', an enclosed piece of land. The suffix Wawen was introduced to distinguish it from other Warwickshire Woottons and comes from Wagen, the Saxon thane who held the land immediately prior to the Norman Conquest.

Wootton Wawen was recorded in the Domesday Book, when St Peter's church stood where it does today. The church still retains

186

its Saxon tower and is set in an immaculate churchyard which won the Diocesan 'Best Kept' competition in 1986 and 1987.

Next to the church stands Wootton Hall, a handsome Italianate stone construction dating from 1637. Until recent times the Hall was owned by Catholic families (principally the Caringtons) and numerous stories and legends have been woven through its history. Mrs Fitzherbert, the morganatic wife of King George IV, spent her childhood at the Hall and visited it after her marriage. The hauntingly perfumed ghost of the Grey Lady, who wanders the Hall, is said to be her.

The Mill, now converted into homes, has played a vital role in the life of the village. In addition to making paper, grinding corn, and generating the Hall's electricity, it was the social centre until the building of the first village hall in 1946.

The former Catholic school adjoins the Mill and, on the Henley side of Wootton is the old village Board school. Both are now converted into private homes and children attend the modern county primary school.

Opposite the Mill is the attractive pink-washed Priory and, as one drives through the village to Birmingham, there are many

The Stratford Canal at Wootton Wawen Basin

picturesque black and white timbered buildings, notably The Bull's Head Inn, the Old Vicarage, and Manor Farm with its unusual and attractive carved plaster door canopy.

Leaving the village on the Stratford side one passes Austy Manor, once a private home and now the headquarters of the British Pregnancy Advisory Service. The Fieldhouse family from Austy endowed the Seymour Homes in memory of their son in Sri Lanka. The homes provide accommodation for elderly residents.

Further out on the edge of the parish boundary is the reconstructed Edstone Hall. It is now a nursing home, but was once the ancestral home of the Somerville family. The poet William Somerville wrote his acclaimed work *The Chase*, while living here. More recently Edstone was a nature cure centre.

Tucked away behind the village shop is Little Croft, once the village workhouse. Along the public footpath across the fields are Blue Hole Cottages, ancient cruck-framed buildings painstakingly restored.

In the past Wootton was principally an agricultural community, with the majority of the population employed on the farms and large estates. A thriving hurdle-making industry was centred on the osier beds.

Although the village has grown it still supports many flourishing farms, a market garden, three garages, two pubs, a retail caravan outlet, canal boat hire business, and a number of successful 'cottage' industries.

Transport has had a great influence over the life of the village. The A34 trunk road cuts a swathe through its centre and a 1960s road-widening scheme deprived Wootton of its Parson's Pond and tree-lined verge. The Stratford Canal, constructed in the late 18th century, is carried in spectacular manner over the A34 by an aqueduct built in 1813. The Stratford to Birmingham railway line also provides Wootton with a vital transport link, although the station is threatened with closure. In the past special trains brought keen anglers in pursuit of their sport, and huge crowds from Birmingham to enjoy the annual flower show.

Index